# NINJA Foodi

**The pressure cooker that crisps.**

## COMPLETE COOKBOOK FOR BEGINNERS

# NINJA Foodi

### The pressure cooker that crisps.

# COMPLETE COOKBOOK FOR BEGINNERS

## Your Expert Guide to Pressure Cook, Air Fry, Dehydrate, and More

### Kenzie Swanhart

Foreword by Justin Warner
Photography by Hélène Dujardin

ROCKRIDGE
PRESS

For general information on our other products and services or to obtain technical support, please contact our Customer Care Department within the U.S. at (866) 744-2665, or outside the U.S. at (510) 253-0500.

Interior Designers: Lisa Schneller Bieser and Debbie Berne
Editor: Talia Platz
Production Editor: Andrew Yackira
Photography: © Hélène Dujardin, 2018
Food Styling: Tami Hardeman
Author Photograph: © Julien Levesque

ISBN: Print 978-1-64152-274-8
eBook 978-1-64152-328-8

To my amazing Ninja Culinary Innovation team for their infinite inspiration and endless support.

# CONTENTS

# FOREWORD

**I am quite possibly the last person** you would expect to write the foreword for this book. I was mentored by Alton Brown, a culinary titan, who has no use for unitaskers that clutter precious counter space. Because of this upbringing in the food biz, I scoffed at the electric pressure cooker craze—my stovetop pressure cooker did the exact same thing! Fueled by millennial bloggers and journalists, fans would ask me about this "new" technology. I would generally refer them to their nearest grandma, as the greatest generation used pressure cooking to tenderize tougher, cheaper cuts of meat. After a while, I became burned out with fielding questions about this "new" device—it seemed to be creating a lot of hype for little reward.

Food Network glam aside, I try to cook for the average cook, and to help them figure out the tools that are worth their investments. So when Kenzie Swanhart and her team of culinary marketers and innovators approached me to "poke holes" in the planning of their new pressure-based cooker, I leaped at the opportunity to vent my frustrations.

When I was introduced to Kenzie, I assumed she would be a salesperson who could cook. I was waiting for her to show me that the device could cut a penny in half. I was completely wrong. Kenzie and her team at Ninja® are innovators in the truest sense of the word. I have never seen anything like it. It's as if, paraphrasing Lewis Carroll, they can do six impossible things before breakfast. It turns out, Kenzie and I were kind of in the same boat when it came to the state of pressure cooking. No stranger to making food approachable and user-friendly, Kenzie has written hundreds of recipes and sold over a hundred thousand cookbooks. She's traversed the blogosphere with the best of them. And she knew exactly where I was coming from when I dumped my grievances on her and her team.

My complaints were as follows:

- Electric pressure cookers do not offer the same control as a stove
- Electric pressure cookers do not create textural juxtaposition
- Electric pressure cookers do not reliably sear
- Electric pressure cookers do not have enough space to manipulate ingredients
- Electric pressure cookers do not deliver restaurant quality results

It took many edible and mental jam sessions, hanging out with engineers, and a recycle bin full of crumpled blueprints, but from this was born the Ninja® Foodi,™ which you now possess, you lucky cook, you.

Kenzie and her team have created something truly new, exciting, helpful, and above all, extremely useful to the home cook and professional alike. The crisping lid of the Foodi, essentially a high-speed convection fan and heating element, is the biggest stroke of culinary genius I have seen in the past decade, if not longer. By having two heat sources, one on top, one on the bottom, along with a crisping basket to regulate the flow of the hot air (no hot and cold spots like your standard oven), the Foodi is essentially an entire kitchen in one device. I could go on and on about the fun things it can do, or how effectively it does those fun things, but the best way for you to experience the Foodi is to use it, and to help with that, Kenzie has written this book.

The recipes herein are tested rigorously. If you follow them, you will succeed. But more importantly, these recipes are designed to unlock the culinary creativity that Kenzie believes is in us all. With very little practice, you and the Foodi will create meals that satisfy more than just hunger. Remember the list of grievances above? Kenzie and her team solved them all. You can sauté just as you would on a stove, but with built in timers and controls that make sense. The crisping lid can broil a steak, just as I would in a professional kitchen, with ease. Broiling creates a crisp crust with a juicy interior. This leads to the aforementioned textural juxtaposition. I could talk about it all day, but the bottom line is this—human beings are hardwired to crave foods with multiple textures. It's good for our brains and makes us happy. In addition, the bottom heating element can effectively sear, which is a claim I don't make lightly. A sear is all or nothing, and it's the difference between crispy yummy skin on a piece of salmon or something that gets scraped off to the side of the plate. I almost forgot, because of the two methods of cooking, a cool new word has been invented—Ninja's TenderCrisp™ cooking. This is how you get a crisp skin on a juicy chicken, or an asparagus spear that is cooked, but not lifeless. It's what restaurants do all the time. In other pressure cookers, none of this is possible. With the Foodi, most everything is.

Kenzie's recipes are the pudding in which the proof is. From Mushroom and Gruyère Tarts (page 56) to Veggie Shepherd's Pie (page 62), not to mention Strawberry Toaster Pastries (page 150) there are tons of epic meals ahead. You and those you feed will be thrilled to have the Foodi in your life and Kenzie by your side. I sure as heck am.

Stay Fresh,
JUSTIN WARNER

# INTRODUCTION

**There are a few unspoken rules** when it comes to cooking dinner. It needs to be quick, it needs to be tasty, and it needs to be good for you. Impossible, right? In the constant hustle and bustle of life, too often we sacrifice at least one of these to get dinner on the table.

It is difficult to find the time to cook, let alone the time it takes to do the dishes, so we reach for the delivery app or settle for a frozen pizza. And when we do cook, we often lack inspiration, falling into the same boring patterns and repeated meals.

What if you could get out of this rut? What if there were a product that enabled you to make quick, healthy, and delicious meals so that you could spend less time cooking and more time doing all of the other things you need to get done?

## What if you had a Ninja® Foodi™?

I have long been a fan of the Ninja brand. When my husband, Julien, and I moved into our first apartment with the tiniest kitchen in America, we purchased the Ninja® Master Prep® Pro System. It did everything from blending smoothies and crushing ice to making frozen drinks, chopping veggies, and tackling every food-processing task we threw at it. It was an incredible little system—emphasis on the word *little*—because, despite all of its talents, I could still store it in a small cabinet in that tiny kitchen. That Ninja product set me off on what became a truly life-altering passion for cooking and helping others cook. I soon started my first blog. Then, while developing recipes for my first book, *Paleo in 28*, the Ninja saved me time and time again, helping me with everything from dressings and sauces to smoothies and whipped cream.

Fast-forward a few years, and I transformed that passion for cooking and helping others cook into a full-time gig when I joined Ninja as the head of the Culinary Marketing and Innovation team. From the moment I walked in the door, I was blown away by the dedication this company has to delivering five-star products that improve people's lives every day. Now we are focused on helping you get dinner done right.

You've likely seen your social media feed flooded recently with pressure cooker recipes. This trend has taken over because pressure cooking delivers on two of the unspoken rules of dinner. It cooks food fast and, because you are using whole ingredients, it is inherently a healthier choice. But the truth is, pressure cooking only takes you so far. It makes juicy, tender food, but there is no texture. And, let's be honest, texture is just as important as flavor.

## Enter the Ninja® Foodi™ the pressure cooker that crisps

The Ninja Foodi delivers a whole new way of cooking by combining the speed of a pressure cooker with the quick-crisping action of an air fryer to give you TenderCrisp™ Technology. Now, quick meals, made from real food and with great flavor and texture, can be on the table in no time—all three rules checked off. And did I mention there is only one pot to clean?

Not only is dinner done right, but now you can make Upside-Down Broccoli and Cheese Quiche (page 26), Crispy Bacon Hash and Baked Eggs (page 25), and even homemade Strawberry Toaster Pastries (page 150) for breakfast. Make snacks and apps like Chili-Ranch Chicken Wings (page 38), Loaded Smashed Potatoes (page 43), and Spinach-Artichoke Bites (page 46). And let's not forget dessert, like my Apple Hand Pies (page 148), Campfire S'Mores (page 151), and Black and Blue Berry Crumble (page 152)—all made using one pot!

Are you hungry yet? Turn on your Ninja Foodi and let's get cooking, because you not only have me to guide you through your journey with it, but I was also part of the team that invented it! I am here to help you get started with this ultimate beginner's guide for this one-of-a-kind cooking adventure that is sure to have everyone leaving the table with happy taste buds and full bellies.

# 1

# Ninja® Foodi™ 101

**Multi-cookers have long been touted** for their versatility and convenience. Slow cookers are the golden example of hands-free cooking. Toss the ingredients into the pot in the morning and come home to a perfectly cooked meal and your house smelling like you've been cooking over the stove all day. Sounds great—but that aroma in the air is flavor that is no longer in your food. Pressure cookers are a step up: They seal in moisture and flavor so that your food is incredibly tender and delicious, and they are exceptionally fast.

But what about texture? Tender food is great, but neither a slow cooker nor a pressure cooker leads to crispy and crunchy texture. What are chicken wings without a crispy exterior? Who wants to eat potpie without a flaky crust?

Enter the Ninja Foodi, a revolutionary appliance that is changing the multi-cooker game!

This chapter introduces you to the only pressure cooker that crisps. I break down all of the functions and benefits of the Ninja Foodi so that you can unleash its full potential—flavor, texture, and speed.

# WHY THE NINJA® FOODI™?

Home cooks have been settling for convenience over flavor, looking to slow cookers and pressure cookers to answer the question "What's for dinner?" With the Ninja Foodi you can have your cake and eat it, too—with frosting, sprinkles, and a scoop of ice cream.

I believe in the Ninja Foodi not only because I helped develop it but also because I use it every day. Even though I have built my career around food, after a long day at work the last thing I want to do is spend hours in the kitchen. The Ninja Foodi is the perfect solution for cooking quick and easy meals in one pot so there is minimal cleanup. I can make things like Lemon Risotto and Roasted Carrots (page 64), Chile-Lime Salmon with Broccoli and Brown Rice (page 76), or Baked Ziti with Meat Sauce (page 130) in about 30 minutes!

When I want to flex my culinary muscles on the weekend or entertain, the Foodi helps me step up my game. I love making appetizers like Crispy Cheesy Arancini (page 39) and Spinach-Artichoke Bites (page 46). And no one can resist my New York Cheesecake (page 154).

## TenderCrisp™ Technology

What is TenderCrisp Technology? First, use Pressure to cook and tenderize food quickly with superheated steam. Then, swap the top and use the Crisping Lid to quickly crisp and caramelize for the perfect finishing touch. It's fantastic for cooking everything—all tender inside and crispy on the outside.

## 360 Meals

Make wholesome meals with multiple components all in one pot. Quickly cook grains on the bottom, add some veggies, and pop in the Reversible Rack and place your proteins on top. Each part of the meal keeps its own unique texture— fluffy rice, roasted veggies, and perfectly cooked proteins. Use the recipes with the 360 Meal label or go off book and try your own combinations.

## One-Pot Wonders

Use TenderCrisp Technology to transform boring soups and stews into One-Pot Wonders. Use Pressure to make your favorite casseroles, stews, chilis, and desserts. Then top with cheese, biscuits, or a crust. Swap the top and use the Crisping Lid to broil the cheese, bake the biscuits, or crisp the crust. Make the recipes that have been handed down from generation to generation, but with this unique twist: You can make them in half the time!

### Frozen to Crispy

The Ninja® Foodi™ can cook food straight from frozen, too. Use Pressure to quickly defrost and tenderize frozen meat, then use the Crisping Lid to crisp the outside. No more uneven defrosting using the microwave or waiting hours for your food to defrost on the counter. Turn frozen chicken and fish into a full 360 Meal, or use frozen fruit to make a scrumptious one-pot fruit crisp.

### Quick-Cue

In the Ninja Foodi you can make restaurant-style barbecue quickly and easily thanks to TenderCrisp™ Technology. Make a rack of ribs, a 5-pound chicken, even brisket and pork belly—tender on the inside with a crispy barbecue bark on the outside. Gone are the days of having to cook in a large smoker or hover over a hot grill waiting for your meat to cook.

## THE FOODI DECONSTRUCTED

Are you getting hungry yet? Before you unlock all of the delicious recipes that the Ninja Foodi now makes possible, let's break down each part of the Foodi, from the two unique lids, to eight cooking functions, and each accessory.

### Pressure Lid

Use the Pressure Lid to turn the Ninja Foodi into the ultimate pressure cooker, cooking and tenderizing food faster than you ever thought possible. You can also turn the pressure release valve from the Seal to the Vent position and Steam your favorite fish and veggies or Slow Cook your favorite stew.

### Crisping Lid

The Crisping Lid adapts the fan and temperature so that you can Air Crisp, Bake/Roast, Broil, and Dehydrate (a feature available on some models). The powerful fan unleashes 2,500 rpms of heated air around your food to crisp and caramelize at up to 450ºF. Use the Crisping Lid after pressure cooking, or use it on its own for the ultimate Air Crisping experience. The Crisping Lid goes as low as 100ºF so that you can dehydrate fruits, veggies, and meats low and slow for yummy, sugar-free snacks.

# How to Convert Recipes to the Ninja® Foodi™ Deluxe

All of the recipes in this cookbook were developed using the 6.5-quart Ninja Foodi. The Ninja Foodi Deluxe has an 8-quart cooking pot. Most of the recipes in this book will work in either one. If using the 8-quart Ninja Foodi, know that these recipes may require a bit more cook time, or an extra shake of the Cook & Crisp™ Basket. For best results, check progress throughout cooking, and shake the basket frequently.

As a good rule of thumb, you can scale up Pressure recipes like soups, stews, and chilies by 50 percent when using the Ninja Foodi Deluxe. You can also fit 50 percent more in the Cook & Crisp Basket.

## Cooking Pot

The Ninja Foodi's cooking pot was specifically designed with an extra-wide diameter so that you can sauté vegetables and sear meats without crowding the pot. Go from Sear/Sauté to Pressure or Slow Cook all in the same pot. Since it is covered in a nano ceramic coating, the cooking pot can handle whatever you want to cook in it. A word of caution, though: Be sure to use silicone or wooden utensils so as not to scratch the pot.

## Cook & Crisp Basket

The Cook & Crisp Basket is designed to make sure that each bite comes out perfectly golden brown and crispy. Use it to Air Crisp crunchy French fries and crispy chicken wings without a ton of oil, or to Dehydrate mangos, apples, and beets. You can use the Cook & Crisp Basket when making any TenderCrisp™ recipe, like finger-licking barbecue or The Perfect Roast Chicken (page 17).

## Reversible Rack

In the lower position, the Reversible Rack allows you to steam veggies and fish quickly and easily. Flip the rack over, and in the higher position it can be used to broil steaks for a crisp crust, or to toast cheesy bread to a perfectly golden brown. In the higher position, the Reversible Rack enables 360 Meals: Place the rack on top of rice, quinoa, or even potatoes, and you can cook a full meal—protein, starch, and a vegetable—in one pot.

# THE NINJA® FOODI™

**Pressure Release Valve**
Easily release pressure.

**Pressure Lid**
Quickly tenderize and cook ingredients.

**Reversible Rack**
Use to steam, or reverse to broil.

**Cook & Crisp™ Basket**
4-quart nonstick, ceramic-coated basket fits 3 lbs of French fries.

**Crisping Lid**
Use to finish off pressure cooked recipes or to air fry your food.

**Cooking Pot**
6.5-quart nonstick, ceramic-coated cooking pot fits a 6-lb roast.

**14 Levels of Safety**
Passed rigorous testing to earn UL safety certification, giving you peace of mind.

# KNOW YOUR FUNCTIONS

Now that you are better acquainted with the Ninja® Foodi™ and its parts and pieces, it is time to learn about all of the different tasks you can accomplish with one pot.

## Pressure

Pressure cooking is a technique that has been used for years to cook food quickly. In fact, you may remember a contraption in your mother's or grand-mother's kitchen that spewed steam as it rattled on the stove. The Ninja Foodi is a far cry from your grandmother's pressure cooker, but the science behind it is the same: Pressurized steam infuses moisture into ingredients and cooks them quickly.

Pressure cooking is ideal for tenderizing tough cuts of meat, quickly cook-ing rice, and everything in between. Simply choose between Low and High pressure, set the cook time, position the pressure release valve in the Seal position, and voilà!

## Steam

Cooking with steam infuses moisture, seals in flavor, and maintains the texture of your food. Steam is the perfect setting for cooking fresh veggies or fish. Simply add water to the cooking pot and place the Reversible Rack in the lower position. Place your food on top of the rack and secure the lid.

## Slow Cook

Contrary to pressure cooking, which is used to quickly cook meats, soups, and stews, the Slow Cook feature builds flavor by braising food low and slow. If you prefer the convenience of tossing your ingredients into a pot in the morning and coming home to a fully cooked meal, then Slow Cook will be your go-to. The Ninja Foodi is equipped with both Low and High slow cooking settings.

## Sear/Sauté

In addition to having plenty of surface area for searing meats and sautéing veggies, the Ninja Foodi also has five stovetop temperature settings. Use the Ninja Foodi just as you would your stove, alternating between Low, Medium Low, Medium, Medium High, and High. Easily go from a gentle simmer to a screaming-hot sear.

### Air Crisp

Ninja's version of air frying, with Air Crisp you can achieve that crispy, crunchy, golden-brown texture we all crave, without all the fat and oil. Use the Air Crisp feature in conjunction with the Cook & Crisp™ Basket to cook your favorite frozen foods, such as French fries, onion rings, and chicken nuggets. Be sure to shake the basket at least once or twice during crisping to ensure the crispiest, most even results. And don't be afraid to sneak a peek under the Crisping Lid and shake often so that you can pull out your food when it is crisped to your liking.

### Bake/Roast

The Ninja® Foodi™ also works as a mini convection oven to cook your favorite baked dishes and roast meats in way less time than in your oven. It takes the Ninja Foodi only 4 to 5 minutes to preheat—far less time than your oven.

Use the Bake/Roast function to make everything from mains, like The Perfect Roast Chicken (page 17), to appetizers and sides, like Crispy Cheesy Arancini (page 39), and even desserts, like Apple Hand Pies (page 148) or New York Cheesecake (page 154).

You can also use this function to reheat leftovers, such as fries, wings, and baked goods that would turn to mush in the microwave.

### Broil

In some parts of the world, the broiler is referred to as a grill. In fact, you can think of the Broil feature on the Ninja Foodi as an upside-down barbecue grill. Broil reaches the hottest temperature of all the Crisping Lid settings and is the easiest way to make meat crispier, cheese cheesier, and life generally better all around. Use Broil to add a crispy, cheesy finish to baked pasta dishes, or reverse-sear your favorite steak for a restaurant-style crisp crust.

With Broil, you are cooking your food directly under very high heat, so be sure to open the lid to sneak a peek frequently so that your food is crisped to your liking and not overdone.

### Dehydrate

There are a variety of different Ninja Foodi models available on the market. Each model is a different size and may have different functionality. Your Ninja Foodi may come with a Dehydrate feature which lowers the fan speed and temperature for optimal dehydrating results. You can make delicious snacks like vegetable chips, dried fruit, and jerky. If you do not have the Dehydrate function, simply skip those recipes and try your hand at one of the other tasty treats in the book!

When you use the Dehydrate feature, the Crisping Lid lowers the fan speed so that you can remove moisture low and slow. Create fruit and veggie chips or re-create your favorite jerky without any added sugar or preservatives.

## FREQUENTLY ASKED QUESTIONS

**Q How do I convert my favorite recipes to the Ninja® Foodi™?**

You can easily convert a number of your favorite recipes to the Ninja Foodi. When converting recipes from a conventional oven, use the Bake/Roast setting and reduce the temperature of the recipe by 25ºF. So if a recipe is baked in the oven at 375ºF, you would set the Ninja Foodi for 350ºF. You will also likely be able to cut down the cook time. Check the food frequently to avoid overcooking.

You can also cook your favorite slow cooker recipes using Pressure so that they cook much quicker. A good rule of thumb is that recipes that slow cook for 8 hours on Low or 4 hours on High should take 25 to 30 minutes in the pressure cooker. It is also important to check your liquid level and ensure that your recipe includes ½ to 1 cup of liquid for the cooker to get to pressure. And as always, make sure the pressure release valve is in the Seal position.

A number of the recipes throughout this book are staples that my husband, Julien, and I have been cooking for years, but with the Ninja Foodi we no longer need to turn on a bunch of appliances and use numerous pots and pans. Instead, recipes like Crispy Chicken Thighs with Roasted Carrots (page 98) are all made in one pot while maintaining their own unique textures. However, every recipe is different, and there is no one rule for doubling or halving all recipes in the book. I recommend trying the recipes as they are and then experimenting with ingredient swaps, cutting recipes in half, or doubling recipes. Note that cook times may change, too.

**Q Why does the Ninja Foodi come with two lids?**

The Ninja Foodi is the only pressure cooker that crisps. For this reason, it comes with a Pressure Lid for the Pressure, Steam, Slow Cook, and Sear/Sauté functions, as well as a Crisping Lid for the Air Crisp, Bake/Roast, Broil, and Dehydrate functions. Use the lids individually or one right after the other to unlock a world of recipes you never knew you could make at home.

**Q  When doing a TenderCrisp™ recipe, should I remove the liquid after using the Pressure Lid, before switching to the Crisping Lid?**

If you are following one of the TenderCrisp recipes in this book, there is no need to remove the liquid before switching to the Crisping Lid. These recipes are specifically designed to work with the amount of liquid in the bottom of the pot.

If you are creating your own recipe and would like to make sure the bottom of your food is browned in the Cook & Crisp™ Basket, make sure not to exceed the 3-cup mark (located on the inside of the pot) with liquid.

**Q  What is the difference between quick release and natural release?**

Quick release is when you manually switch the pressure release valve to the Vent position. Quick release is used in the majority of this book's recipes. Natural release occurs when you let the Ninja® Foodi™ decrease in pressure naturally after cooking is complete. This technique is most commonly used when cooking beans.

**Q  If I don't have all of the ingredients called for in a recipe, can I swap in an ingredient I do have?**

I have added tips throughout these recipes with ingredient swaps and suggestions. If the recipe you are making doesn't have a recipe swap noted, confirm first that the swap you want to make will cook in the same amount of time as the original ingredient (see the charts on page 159). Some swaps are easier to make than others, like swapping elbow pasta for cavatappi pasta, while other ingredient changes may require adjusting cook times and temperatures. My advice is to experiment and have fun. After all, that's how I created all of these recipes!

**Q  Can I cook frozen food in the Ninja Foodi?**

Yes! One of the best things about the Ninja Foodi is that you can cook frozen food straight from the freezer without the need to defrost. Use Pressure to turn frozen chicken breasts into shredded chicken or ground beef into chili, or use the combination of Pressure and the Crisping Lid to roast a whole chicken from frozen or cook the perfect medium-rare steak. Follow the charts at the back of the book (see page 159) for cook times for specific foods.

# 2

# Start Cooking!

**You are about to discover** a whole new way of cooking that is sure to inspire you to try a host of new recipes and techniques in the kitchen. Whether you are a novice in the kitchen or a seasoned chef, you are sure to be impressed with what you can accomplish in the Ninja® Foodi,™ the pressure cooker that crisps. You don't even need to know how to boil water to whip up a delicious meal that everyone is sure to love.

The Ninja Foodi makes it easy to put breakfast, lunch, and dinner on the table—as well as delicious snacks and desserts. You can make Hardboiled Eggs (page 23), Apple-Cranberry Oatmeal (page 29), and Banana Bread French Toast (page 30) for breakfast, and mouthwatering snacks and appetizers like Beet Chips (page 36), Chili-Ranch Chicken Wings (page 38), and Buffalo Chicken Meatballs (page 41). How about Lemon Risotto and Roasted Carrots (page 64), Orange Chicken and Broccoli (page 102), or Barbecue Pork Chops (page 128) for dinner? And I didn't forget about dessert: Cinnamon-Sugar Bites (page 146), Black and Blue Berry Crumble (page 152), and Peanut Butter and Chocolate Lava Cakes (page 156) can all be prepared with the Ninja Foodi.

# GETTING YOUR KITCHEN READY

One of the best things about the Ninja® Foodi™ is that you don't even need a kitchen to cook a full meal. Take it from me: You can cook a whole roast chicken worthy of a holiday dinner table from your hotel room. I have the pictures to prove it!

While you don't need a bunch of equipment or specialty food, there are a few staples that will help you get the most out of your Ninja Foodi. Here is what I always have in my refrigerator and pantry so that I can cook a quick dinner or whip up a snack in no time.

## Super-Simple Staples

**All-purpose flour:** Large mason jars filled with flour sit in on my counter so that they are easily accessible while I cook. I keep a variety of flours on hand, but if you are going to have only one, it should be all-purpose flour. Used for everything from biscuits and cookies to thickening sauces, this pantry staple lasts up to a year when stored in an airtight container.

**Bread crumbs:** Perfect for topping casseroles and breading chicken. You can buy a prepackaged brand or save some money and make your own. Wheat, white, multigrain, or rye breads can all be turned into fresh toasted bread crumbs with minimal effort.

**Broths/stocks:** These are an easy way to add extra flavor to any recipe you make in the Ninja Foodi. Simply use vegetable, chicken, or beef broth or stock in place of any water called for in the recipe.

**Butter:** While we always have a stick or two of butter in the refrigerator, I also keep a few spares in the freezer—just in case. Mix butter with bread crumbs or cut butter into piecrust dough, and you will be delighted by not only the flavor it brings to the dish but also how it aids in browning and creating the flaky piecrusts and biscuits that top your favorite casseroles. I prefer to use unsalted butter to better control the amount of sodium in my recipes. The recipes in this book all use unsalted butter.

**Canned tomatoes:** Whole, diced, puréed—tomatoes add acidity, sweetness, and color to a vast array of dishes. It is impractical to assume that you will always have fresh tomatoes available, but canned tomatoes provide consistent flavor, especially when fresh ones are out of season. Use canned tomatoes for sauces, stews, and soups.

**Dry pasta:** Whether you prefer penne, rigatoni, or cavatappi, having dry pasta in your pantry means you're always prepared for an impromptu meal. Dry pasta is versatile and can be paired with ragùs, soups, and casseroles so you can make a meal with whatever fresh ingredients you have on hand.

**Eggs:** Whether you keep them in the refrigerator or on the counter, always have a carton of large eggs readily available.

**Extra-virgin olive oil (EVOO):** Just like with flour, I keep a variety of oils in the pantry, but EVOO is the hero of most meals. A good olive oil can be used for sautéing, finishing, and everything else in between.

**Garlic:** There are three staples that I use in almost every recipe throughout this book: Olive oil, sea salt, and freshly ground black pepper. If I had to choose a fourth, it would be garlic. Sauté garlic in oil before pressure cooking to pack a punch of flavor in any meal.

**Lemons:** There aren't many fresh foods on my list of pantry staples, but having lemons available for freshly squeezed juice is a must. And the zest can add brightness to many a dish.

**Lentils and beans:** Relatively inexpensive and super easy to make, lentils and beans add extra protein, fiber, and a bit of bulk to any dish.

**Onions:** Almost every great meal begins with sautéing an onion. Don't worry about keeping all varieties on the counter—a few yellow onions are versatile enough to cook with in most recipes.

**Parmesan cheese:** A small amount packs a lot of flavor. Don't waste your time with pre-grated cheese; buy a wedge and it will last awhile in the refrigerator.

**Piecrust:** Save yourself time and effort. Refrigerated piecrust can be just as buttery, flaky, and delicious as homemade. Keep a roll in the refrigerator, and you will always be prepared for impromptu casseroles and desserts.

**Whole grains:** Rice, oats, and quinoa make a satisfying base for any meal and work for breakfast, lunch, dinner, and dessert. Oats can also be tossed with sugar and butter to turn frozen or fresh fruit into an epic dessert crumble.

## Super-Simple Spice Rack

**Basil:** Dried basil is delicious in sauces and as a seasoning on chicken and other meats.

**Bay leaves:** Use fresh or dried bay leaves to add a depth of flavor to soups, stews, and sauces. Always remember to remove and discard the leaves before serving.

**Black pepper:** My recipes always specify freshly ground black pepper because freshly ground peppercorns give you the fullest flavor. I have a grinder that is always next to the stove and is constantly being refilled.

**Cayenne pepper:** Cayenne is ground from one of the hottest varietals of dried hot peppers and is often optional in recipes. Use it sparingly to add a little spice to your dish.

**Garlic powder:** This is simply ground dehydrated garlic. Mix with salt, and you have garlic salt. Keep garlic powder in the spice rack to season a variety of pasta, veggie, and chicken dishes. It is also used in several spice blends.

**Ground cinnamon:** Known for its warm, sweet flavor, cinnamon is often used in baked goods but can also be the unexpected ingredient in stews and sauces.

**Ground cumin:** Cumin is a popular aromatic spice in Middle Eastern, Asian, Mediterranean, and Mexican cuisines.

**Onion powder:** Like garlic powder, onion powder is made from ground dehydrated onions and is used on its own as well as in a number of spice blends.

**Oregano:** This is classified as either Mediterranean or Mexican and is often used to season dishes from these two regions.

**Paprika:** This spice is ground from dried red bell peppers. There are different types of paprika, including smoked and sweet.

**Sea salt:** Salt adds flavor to any recipe. It is used in both the sweet and savory recipes throughout this book. Remember, when cooking, table salt cannot be substituted 1:1 for sea salt, as it is much finer and will result in an oversalted dish. Use a little, taste, and adjust with more if it's needed.

# No Recipe? No Problem.

Don't have the ingredients on hand to make a specific recipe? I've got you covered. Follow the simple combinations below to prepare effortless and delicious meals in your Foodi™ with less than 5 ingredients.

Still can't find what you are looking for? Take a look at the charts in the back of the book. Make sure the time to cook the grains and protein under Pressure are a match and then sub in your favorite veggies on top of the grain or on the Reversible Rack.

| STEP 1 | STEP 2 | STEP 3 | STEP 4 | STEP 5 | STEP 6 | STEP 7 |
|---|---|---|---|---|---|---|
| Place grain or starch & liquid in pot | Place protein on Reversible Rack (in broil position) | Assemble Pressure Lid | Quick release pressure; carefully remove lid | Add a vegetable (tossed with 1 tablespoon oil plus salt & pepper to taste) | Brush protein with sauce or coat with spice rub of your choice | Broil for 10 minutes |
| 1 cup long-grain brown rice & 1 cup chicken broth | 2 (9- to 16-oz) boneless chicken breasts | Pressure cook for 5 minutes | | On top of grain or starch: | Adobo | |
| 1 lb whole baby red potatoes & ½ cup water | | | | 1 head broccoli, cut in small florets | Barbecue | |
| 1 cup green or brown lentils & 1 cup chicken broth | 1 lb frozen chicken wings | | | | Pesto | |
| 1 cup red quinoa & 1 cup chicken broth | 1 lb frozen meatballs | | | 1 (12-oz) bag green beans | Sweet & Sour | |
| | | | | 1 bunch asparagus, trimmed | Teriyaki | |
| 1 cup farro & 1 cup chicken broth | 4 (6- to 8-oz) frozen boneless, skinless chicken breasts | Pressure cook for 10 minutes | | | | |
| 1 cup short-grain brown rice & 1 cup chicken broth | | | | | | |
| 1 cup pearl barley & 1 cup chicken broth | 4 (6- to 8-oz) frozen bone-in, skin-on chicken thighs | | | | | |
| 2 whole sweet potatoes & ½ cup water | | | | | | |

# THE NINJA® FOODI™ STEP BY STEP

There's no need to feel intimidated when you first get your Ninja Foodi home and open the box. To acquaint yourself with the appliance, start by trying out a few recipes that use only one or two of its cooking functions, like my Apple-Cranberry Oatmeal (page 29), Loaded Smashed Potatoes (page 43), or Pita Bread Pizza with Sausage and Peppers (page 126). I specifically recommend familiarizing yourself with the Pressure and Air Crisp functions (check out the cooking charts on page 159). Once you feel comfortable, put the two techniques together, as this is where the real magic happens!

On the opposite page is my recipe for The Perfect Roast Chicken. In it, I use Pressure to quickly cook and tenderize the chicken. This ensures that the chicken is moist and flavorful. Then I swap the tops and use Air Crisp to give the bird a crispy, golden-brown finish for the perfect roast chicken every time. The best part is, this recipe takes less than 45 minutes start to finish!

I've broken down the recipe below step by step in a bit more detail than the other recipes throughout the book in the hopes that it will answer all of your questions and get you better acquainted with the Ninja Foodi.

Note that in this recipe I use the Cook & Crisp™ Basket in both steps so that I do not need to do anything more than swap the top to go from Pressure to Air Crisp. When you've finished, you'll be enjoying a perfectly roasted chicken!

## ABOUT THE RECIPES

The following chapters are filled with simple yet flavorful recipes designed to help you jump-start your Ninja® Foodi™ adventure. Created to show you how to use the Ninja Foodi to elevate your everyday meals, the recipes use common ingredients to make incredible meals quickly and with wonderful flavor and delightful textures. In fact, there are 40 recipes that can be made in under 30 minutes. There are all types of recipes, whether you're looking for meal suggestions, including breakfast, snacks, and appetizers, or if you're a meat lover or want to satisfy the vegetarian in your family. And don't forget dessert!

Each recipe includes dietary labels to indicate if it is Dairy-Free, Gluten-Free (always check ingredient packaging for gluten-free labeling), Nut-Free, Vegan, or Vegetarian. You will also see labels for recipes that are Under 30 Minutes, and 360 Meals that include a protein, starch, and vegetable. All recipes also include nutritional information.

*(continued on page 19)*

# The Perfect Roast Chicken

1 (4½- to 5-pound) whole chicken

½ cup white wine

Juice of 1 lemon

1 tablespoon sea salt, plus 1 teaspoon

5 garlic cloves, minced, divided

1 tablespoon extra-virgin olive oil

4 tablespoons (½ stick) unsalted butter, melted

1 teaspoon freshly ground black pepper

1 tablespoon minced fresh rosemary

**PREP TIME**
10 MINUTES

**TOTAL COOK TIME**
42 MINUTES

**APPROX. PRESSURE BUILD**
6 MINUTES

**PRESSURE COOK**
20 MINUTES

**PRESSURE RELEASE**
1 MINUTE

**AIR CRISP**
15 MINUTES

**ACCESSORIES**
COOK & CRISP™ BASKET, PRESSURE LID, CRISPING LID

1. Discard the neck from inside the chicken cavity and remove any excess fat and leftover feathers. Rinse the chicken inside and out and tie the legs together with cooking twine.

2. Combine the wine, lemon juice, 1 tablespoon of sea salt, and 3 tablespoons of minced garlic in the cooking pot.

3. Place the chicken in the Cook & Crisp™ Basket and place the basket in the pot.

4. Assemble the Pressure Lid, making sure the pressure release valve is in the Seal position. Select Pressure and set to High (HI). Set the time to 20 minutes, then select Start/Stop to begin.

*Note: It will take about 6 minutes to build pressure. You will know the pressure is built when the red indicator on the lid pops up and the timer begins to count down.*

5. When pressure cooking is complete, carefully turn the pressure release valve to the Vent position to quick release the pressure. When the unit has finished releasing the pressure, carefully remove the Pressure Lid.

6. In a small bowl, combine the olive oil, melted butter, and remaining garlic. Brush the mixture over the chicken and season it with the remaining 1 teaspoon of salt and the pepper. ➤

7. Close the Crisping Lid. Select Air Crisp, set the temperature to 400°F, and set the time to 15 minutes. Select Start/Stop to begin.

*Note: The timer will begin to count down immediately. Don't be afraid to lift the lid and sneak a peek to ensure that the food is crisping to your liking. The Ninja® Foodi™ will recover its temperature quickly, so you will not interrupt cooking.*

8. After about 10 minutes, lift the Crisping Lid and sprinkle the chicken with the fresh rosemary. Close the Crisping Lid and continue cooking. If you prefer a crispier chicken, add an additional 5-10 minutes.

9. Cooking is complete when the internal temperature of the chicken registers 165°F on a meat thermometer inserted into the thickest part of the meat (it should not touch the bone). Carefully remove the chicken from the basket using the Ninja Roast Lifters or 2 large serving forks.

10. Let the chicken rest for 10 minutes before carving and serving.

**Per serving** Calories: 418; Total fat: 30g; Saturated fat: 12g; Cholesterol: 139mg; Sodium: 1845mg; Carbohydrates: 2g; Fiber: 0g; Protein: 31g

# 7 Tips for the Perfect TenderCrisp™

It's the TenderCrisp Technology that sets the Ninja® Foodi™ apart from every other product out there. Here are seven basic, simple steps to get that tender and crispy finish every time you use your Foodi.

**Heat it up.** When using the Sear/Sauté, Air Crisp, or Broil functions, always preheat the Ninja Foodi for 5 minutes before adding food. This will ensure that you have reached the correct temperature before you begin to cook.

**Shake it up.** It is recommended to always shake (or toss with tongs) food that is layered on top of itself in the Cook & Crisp™ Basket at least once or twice during crisping. But the more you shake or toss, the more even and crispy the result will be.

**Spritz with oil.** Use a bottle with a nozzle or a cooking spray can to evenly coat large proteins and veggies with oil. You can also use a brush if you're applying thick sauces and marinades.

**Keep it consistent.** Foods that are the same size cook more evenly. Be sure to cut foods into similar-size pieces when prepping a recipe.

**Rinse the rice.** When using Pressure to cook rice and grains, for best results be sure to rinse them thoroughly, until the water runs clear.

**Keep it separate.** When following recipes for a 360 Meal, you will layer meats over veggies and rice using the Reversible Rack. This builds flavor and keeps the meal in one pot, all while maintaining texture. If you prefer to keep the meat drippings separate, place aluminum foil over the Revesible Rack before adding the meat.

**Utensils matter.** Keep your Ninja Foodi looking and performing its best by only using wooden, silicone, or silicone-tipped utensils.

To help guide you through the recipes as you get started with the Ninja Foodi, I have outlined the total time it takes to cook the recipe from start to finish with clear specifics, so important steps like pressure build and pressure release aren't forgotten. I have also noted which Ninja Foodi accessories and lids are used so that you'll know what you'll need for each recipe.

As you begin, remember to read through each recipe completely and gather all the ingredients you need in advance. As with everything else, a little prep work before you begin to cook will save you time in the long run.

I also suggest that you follow each recipe exactly as written your first time trying it. Then, as you become more comfortable with the Ninja Foodi, you can switch things up and try swapping ingredients.

Above all else, remember to have fun! So what are you waiting for? It's time to get cooking with the Ninja Foodi!

# 3

# Breakfast

Left: Apple-Cranberry Oatmeal, page 29

# Homemade Yogurt

**SERVES 8**

*Unlike with other multi-cookers, you don't need a specific button to make yogurt in the Ninja® Foodi.™ To get started you will need a "yogurt starter," or 2 tablespoons of yogurt with active live cultures, and a thermometer. I use vanilla and honey to flavor and sweeten the yogurt. Jam, fruit purée, and extracts also provide great flavors. Or top plain yogurt with berries or granola for both flavor and texture. Refrigerate leftovers for up to 2 weeks.*

**½ gallon whole milk**

**2 tablespoons plain yogurt with active live cultures**

**1 tablespoon vanilla extract (optional)**

**½ cup honey (optional)**

1. Pour the milk into the pot. Assemble the Pressure Lid, making sure the pressure release valve is in the Vent position. Select Sear/Sauté and set to Medium. Select Start/Stop to begin.

2. Bring the milk to 180ºF, checking the temperature often and stirring frequently so the milk does not burn at the bottom. Select Start/Stop to turn off Sear/Sauté.

3. Allow the milk to cool to 110ºF, continuing to check the temperature often and stirring frequently. Gently skim off the "skin" on the milk and discard.

4. Stir in the yogurt and whisk until incorporated.

5. Assemble the Pressure Lid, making sure the pressure release valve is in the Seal position. Select Keep Warm and let sit for 8 hours.

6. After 8 hours, transfer the yogurt to a glass container and chill for 4 hours in the refrigerator.

7. Add the vanilla and honey (if using) to the yogurt and mix until well combined. Cover and place the glass bowl back in the refrigerator, or divide the yogurt among airtight glass jars.

**PREP TIME**
15 MINUTES

**TOTAL TIME**
12 HOURS

**ACCESSORIES**
PRESSURE LID

**GLUTEN-FREE, NUT-FREE, VEGETARIAN**

**TIP:** If you prefer a thicker Greek-style yogurt, let the yogurt strain through cheesecloth into a large mixing bowl overnight in the refrigerator.

**Per serving** Calories: 149; Total fat: 8g; Saturated fat: 5g; Cholesterol: 25mg; Sodium: 99mg; Carbohydrates: 13g; Fiber: 0g; Protein: 8g

# Hardboiled Eggs

*Perhaps one of the first things people learn to do in the kitchen, after making a bowl of cereal, is boiling a pot of water. With a pressure cooker, the temperature inside the pot reaches above the boiling point, and superheated steam is used to cook foods quickly and evenly. In my opinion, cooking hardboiled eggs with steam improves the texture of the eggs and makes them much easier to peel.*

**1 cup water**　　　　　　　**2 to 12 eggs**

1. Place the Reversible Rack in the pot in the lower position. Add the water and arrange the eggs on the rack in a single layer.

2. Assemble the Pressure Lid, making sure the pressure release valve is in the Seal position. Select Pressure and set to Low. Set the time to 8 minutes. Select Start/Stop to begin.

3. While the eggs are cooking, prepare a large bowl of ice water.

4. When pressure cooking is complete, quick release the pressure by moving the pressure release valve to the Vent position. Carefully remove the lid when the unit has finished releasing pressure.

5. Using a slotted spoon, immediately transfer the eggs to the ice water bath and allow to cool for 5 minutes.

**Per serving (1 egg)** Calories: 71; Total fat: 5g; Saturated fat: 2g; Cholesterol: 211mg; Sodium: 70mg; Carbohydrates: 0g; Fiber: 0g; Protein: 6g

**PREP TIME**
2 MINUTES

**TOTAL COOK TIME**
15 MINUTES

**APPROX. PRESSURE BUILD**
6 MINUTES

**PRESSURE COOK**
8 MINUTES

**PRESSURE RELEASE**
1 MINUTE

**ACCESSORIES**
REVERSIBLE RACK, PRESSURE LID

**DAIRY-FREE, GLUTEN-FREE, NUT-FREE, VEGETARIAN, UNDER 30 MINUTES**

**TIP:** Hardboiled eggs with hard yolks are ideal for deviled eggs, but if you prefer runny yolks, then you'll want softboiled eggs. For softboiled eggs, cook on Low for 2 to 3 minutes, and for medium-boiled eggs, cook on Low for 5 to 6 minutes.

# Easy Cheesy Egg Bake

**SERVES 4**

*I think of this egg bake as a formula more than an actual recipe because I can easily switch it up with my favorite ingredients. I always have eggs, milk, and cheese in the refrigerator, and I often change up the protein and veggies depending on what we have on hand. Made in just a few minutes and with little effort, it's a smart choice for breakfast or an effortless dinner on nights when you don't know what to cook.*

4 eggs
1 cup milk
1 teaspoon sea salt
1 teaspoon freshly ground black pepper

1 cup shredded Cheddar cheese
1 red bell pepper, seeded and chopped
8 ounces ham, chopped
1 cup water

**PREP TIME**
5 MINUTES

**TOTAL COOK TIME**
27 MINUTES

**APPROX. PRESSURE BUILD**
6 MINUTES

**PRESSURE COOK**
20 MINUTES

**PRESSURE RELEASE**
1 MINUTE

**ACCESSORIES**
REVERSIBLE RACK, PRESSURE LID

**GLUTEN-FREE, NUT-FREE, UNDER 30 MINUTES**

1. In a medium mixing bowl, whisk together the eggs, milk, salt, and black pepper. Stir in the Cheddar cheese.

2. Place the bell pepper and ham in the Multi-Purpose Pan or an 8-inch baking pan. Pour the egg mixture over the pepper and ham. Cover the pan with aluminum foil and place on the Reversible Rack.

3. Pour the water into the pot. Place the rack with the pan in the pot in the lower position.

4. Assemble the Pressure Lid, making sure the pressure release valve is in the Seal position. Select Pressure and set to High. Set the time to 20 minutes. Select Start/Stop to begin.

5. When pressure cooking is complete, quick release the pressure by moving the pressure release valve to the Vent position. Carefully remove the lid when the unit has finished releasing pressure.

6. When cooking is complete, remove the pan from the pot and place it on a cooling rack. Let cool for 5 minutes, then serve.

**TIP:** Swap the red bell pepper for other veggies like broccoli, spinach, and onions, but stay away from those that will release water, like tomatoes, zucchini, and mushrooms. Chicken and smoked sausage make good substitutes for the ham.

**Per serving** Calories: 332; Total fat: 21g; Saturated fat: 10g; Cholesterol: 280mg; Sodium: 1693mg; Carbohydrates: 6g; Fiber: 1g; Protein: 28g

# Crispy Bacon Hash and Baked Eggs

**SERVES 4**

*The best kind of hash browns are crispy and crunchy; soggy potatoes have no business being at brunch. This recipe uses both the bottom and top heating elements in the Ninja® Foodi™ to ensure that every element of the dish is cooked to perfection—crunchy bacon, caramelized onions, crispy potatoes, and baked eggs. Plus, all of the ingredients cook in one pot, so cleanup is a breeze.*

**6 slices bacon, chopped**

**1 yellow onion, diced**

**2 russet potatoes, peeled and diced**

**1 teaspoon paprika**

**1 teaspoon sea salt**

**1 teaspoon freshly ground black pepper**

**1 teaspoon garlic salt**

**4 eggs**

**PREP TIME**
10 MINUTES

**TOTAL COOK TIME**
40 MINUTES

**SEAR/SAUTÉ**
5 MINUTES

**BAKE/ROAST**
35 MINUTES

**ACCESSORIES**
CRISPING LID

**DAIRY-FREE, GLUTEN-FREE, NUT-FREE**

1. Select Sear/Sauté and set to Medium High. Select Start/Stop to begin. Allow the pot to preheat for 5 minutes.

2. Once hot, add the bacon to the pot. Cook, stirring occasionally, for 5 minutes, or until the bacon is crispy.

3. Add the onion and potatoes to the pot. Sprinkle with the paprika, sea salt, pepper, and garlic salt.

4. Close the Crisping Lid. Select Bake/Roast, set the temperature to 350ºF, and set the time to 25 minutes. Cook, stirring occasionally, until the potatoes are tender and golden brown.

5. Crack the eggs onto the surface of the hash. Close the Crisping Lid. Select Bake/Roast, set the temperature to 350ºF, and set the time to 10 minutes.

6. Check the eggs after 3 minutes. Continue cooking for the remaining 7 minutes, checking occasionally, until your desired doneness is achieved. Serve immediately.

**Per serving** Calories: 364; Total fat: 24g; Saturated fat: 8g; Cholesterol: 240mg; Sodium: 1008mg; Carbohydrates: 24g; Fiber: 2g; Protein: 14g

# Upside-Down Broccoli and Cheese Quiche

*Flip breakfast on its head with this unique twist on an old favorite. I love the classic combination of broccoli and Cheddar in this recipe. Paired with a buttery, flaky crust, this quiche is sure to have everyone around the table asking for more.*

8 eggs
½ cup milk
1 teaspoon sea salt
1 teaspoon freshly ground black pepper
1 cup shredded Cheddar cheese

1 tablespoon extra-virgin olive oil
1 yellow onion, chopped
2 garlic cloves, minced
2 cups thinly sliced broccoli florets
1 refrigerated piecrust, at room temperature

**PREP TIME**
10 MINUTES

**TOTAL COOK TIME**
20 MINUTES

**SEAR/SAUTÉ**
10 MINUTES

**BROIL**
10 MINUTES

**ACCESSORIES**
CRISPING LID

**NUT-FREE, VEGETARIAN, UNDER 30 MINUTES**

1. Select Sear/Sauté and set to High. Select Start/Stop to begin. Allow the pot to preheat for 5 minutes.

2. In a large mixing bowl, whisk together the eggs, milk, salt, and pepper. Stir in the Cheddar cheese.

3. Put the oil, onion, and garlic in the preheated pot and stir occasionally for 5 minutes. Add the broccoli florets and sauté for another 5 minutes.

4. Pour the egg mixture over the vegetables and gently stir for 1 minute (this will allow the egg mixture to temper well and ensure that it cooks evenly under the crust).

5. Lay the piecrust evenly on top of the filling mixture, folding over the edges if necessary. Make a small cut in the center of the piecrust so that steam can escape during baking.

6. Close the Crisping Lid. Select Broil and set the time to 10 minutes. Select Start/Stop to begin.

7. When cooking is complete, remove the pot and place it on a heat-resistant surface. Let the quiche rest for 5 to 10 minutes before serving.

**Per serving** Calories: 393; Total fat: 26g; Saturated fat: 10g; Cholesterol: 304mg; Sodium: 773mg; Carbohydrates: 26g; Fiber: 2g; Protein: 16g

# Simple Strawberry Jam

*I love making jam and then using it throughout the week on toast and biscuits, stirred into oatmeal and Homemade Yogurt (page 22), or as a topping for pancakes and French toast. Here I use 2 pounds of strawberries, but you can use blueberries, raspberries, blackberries, or a berry mix! Have fun, and make this recipe your own. You can also cut the recipe in half or double it depending on how much jam you need.*

**2 pounds strawberries, hulled and halved**

**Juice of 2 lemons**
**1½ cups granulated sugar**

1. Place the strawberries, lemon juice, and sugar in the pot. Using a silicone potato masher, mash the ingredients together to begin to release the strawberry juices.

2. Assemble the Pressure Lid, making sure the pressure release valve is in the Seal position. Select Pressure and set to High. Set the time to 1 minute. Select Start/Stop to begin.

3. When pressure cooking is complete, allow the pressure to naturally release for 10 minutes, then quick release any remaining pressure by moving the pressure release valve to the Vent position. Carefully remove the lid when the pressure has finished releasing.

4. Select Sear/Sauté and set to Medium High. Select Start/Stop to begin. Allow the jam to reduce for 20 minutes, or until it tightens.

5. Mash the strawberries using the silicone potato masher for a textured jam, or transfer the strawberry mixture to a food processor and purée for a smooth consistency. Let the jam cool, pour it into a glass jar, and refrigerate for up to 2 weeks.

**Per serving (1 tablespoon)** Calories: 23; Total fat: 0g; Saturated fat: 0g; Cholesterol: 0mg; Sodium: 0mg; Carbohydrates: 6g; Fiber: 0g; Protein: 0g

**PREP TIME**
10 MINUTES

**TOTAL COOK TIME**
42 MINUTES

**APPROX. PRESSURE BUILD**
10 MINUTES

**PRESSURE COOK**
1 MINUTE

**PRESSURE RELEASE**
11 MINUTES

**SEAR/SAUTÉ**
20 MINUTES

**ACCESSORIES**
PRESSURE LID

**DAIRY-FREE, GLUTEN-FREE, NUT-FREE, VEGAN**

**TIP:** This natural jam may be a bit looser than store-bought versions because it uses all whole ingredients. If you prefer to thicken the jam, stir in flavorless gelatin after step 4.

# Apple-Cranberry Oatmeal

**SERVES 4**

*A bowl of warm oatmeal is the perfect way to start the day, but in the morning there is no time to babysit the pot on the stove. Now you can cook the oatmeal in minutes—no baby-sitting required. I love the combination of apples and cranberries because it feels like fall, but you can change the flavor based on what you have in the pantry. Try strawberries and coconut flakes, chocolate chips and peanut butter, or blueberries and brown sugar.*

**2 cups gluten-free steel-cut oats**

**3¾ cups water**

**¼ cup apple cider vinegar**

**1 tablespoon ground cinnamon**

**½ teaspoon ground nutmeg**

**½ teaspoon vanilla extract**

**½ cup dried cranberries, plus more for garnish**

**2 apples, peeled, cored, and diced**

**⅛ teaspoon sea salt**

**Maple syrup, for topping**

1. Add the oats, water, vinegar, cinnamon, nutmeg, vanilla, cranberries, apples, and salt to the pot. Assemble the Pressure Lid, making sure the pressure release valve is in the Seal position. Select Pressure and set to High. Set the time to 11 minutes. Select Start/Stop to begin.

2. When pressure cooking is complete, allow the pressure to naturally release for 10 minutes, then quick release any remaining pressure by moving the pressure release valve to the Vent position. Carefully remove the lid when the pressure has finished releasing.

3. Stir the oatmeal and serve immediately. Top with maple syrup and more dried cranberries, as desired.

**Per serving** Calories: 399; Total fat: 6g; Saturated fat: 1g; Cholesterol: 0mg; Sodium: 76mg; Carbohydrates: 71g; Fiber: 12g; Protein: 14g

**PREP TIME**
5 MINUTES

**TOTAL COOK TIME**
27 MINUTES

**APPROX. PRESSURE BUILD**
5 MINUTES

**PRESSURE COOK**
11 MINUTES

**PRESSURE RELEASE**
11 MINUTES

**ACCESSORIES**
PRESSURE LID

**DAIRY-FREE, GLUTEN-FREE, NUT-FREE, VEGAN, UNDER 30 MINUTES**

**TIP:** If you prefer old-fashioned oats, you can substitute an equal amount of them for the steel-cut oats and reduce pressure cook time to 6 minutes. You can also add more water if you prefer a thinner oatmeal.

# Banana Bread French Toast

**SERVES 4**

*Growing up I always preferred to have a sweet breakfast over something savory, because who would choose an omelet over a Belgian waffle covered in maple syrup, whipped cream, and sprinkles? That would be like choosing breakfast over dessert! While my preferences have changed a bit over the years, I still like to treat myself to a sweet breakfast once in a while, and when I do, French toast is my favorite. The warm cinnamon paired with sweet maple syrup gets me every time. But what makes the perfect French toast is a soft bread center and a crispy exterior. This recipe has it all.*

**3 eggs**

**¼ cup milk**

**1 tablespoon granulated sugar**

**1 teaspoon vanilla extract**

**1 teaspoon ground cinnamon**

**Nonstick cooking spray**

**6 slices French bread, cut into 1-inch cubes, divided**

**3 bananas, sliced into rounds, divided**

**2 tablespoons brown sugar, divided**

**¼ cup cream cheese, at room temperature**

**½ cup water**

**2 tablespoons cold unsalted butter, sliced**

**¼ cup chopped pecans (optional)**

**2 tablespoons maple syrup**

**PREP TIME**
15 MINUTES

**TOTAL COOK TIME**
35 MINUTES

**APPROX. PRESSURE BUILD**
8 MINUTES

**PRESSURE COOK**
20 MINUTES

**PRESSURE RELEASE**
2 MINUTES

**BAKE/ROAST**
5 MINUTES

**ACCESSORIES**
REVERSIBLE RACK,
PRESSURE LID, CRISPING LID

**VEGETARIAN**

1. In a medium mixing bowl, whisk together the eggs, milk, granulated sugar, vanilla, and cinnamon.

2. Grease the Multi-Purpose Pan or an 8-inch baking pan with cooking spray and arrange half the bread cubes in the pan in a single layer. Layer half the banana slices over the bread and sprinkle with 1 tablespoon of brown sugar.

3. Spread the cream cheese on top of the bread and bananas. Layer the remaining bread cubes on top of the cream cheese, layer the remaining banana slices on top of the bread, and sprinkle with the remaining 1 tablespoon of brown sugar.

4. Pour the egg mixture over the bread mixture, coating the bread completely.

5. Pour the water into the pot. Place the pan on the Reversible Rack, making sure the rack is in the lower position, then place the rack with the pan in the pot. Assemble the Pressure Lid, making sure the pressure release valve is in the Seal position. Select Pressure and set to High. Set the time to 20 minutes. Select Start/Stop to begin.

6. When pressure cooking is complete, quick release the pressure by moving the pressure release valve to the Vent position. Carefully remove the lid when the pressure has finished releasing.

7. Top the French toast with the sliced butter, pecans (if using), and maple syrup.

8. Close the Crisping Lid. Select Bake/Roast, set the temperature to 390ºF, and set the time to 5 minutes.

9. Check the doneness and add more time as needed until your desired crispiness is achieved. Serve immediately.

**Per serving** Calories: 448; Total fat: 16g; Saturated fat: 8g; Cholesterol: 191mg; Sodium: 461mg; Carbohydrates: 66g; Fiber: 4g; Protein: 13g

# 4

# Snacks & Appetizers

Left: Chili-Ranch Chicken Wings, page 38

# Watermelon Jerky

*I never quite understood when people described fruit as nature's candy. Don't get me wrong, I love a crisp apple or a juicy orange, but let's be honest—it's not the same as a sugary-sweet treat. Enter dehydrated fruit. This watermelon jerky is intensely sweet like your favorite hard candy and chewy like taffy, only better. Not only is this a crave-worthy snack, it is also a perfect topper when crumbled over a salad or soup.*

**1 cup seedless watermelon (1-inch) cubes**

1. Arrange the watermelon cubes in a single layer in the Cook & Crisp Basket. Place the basket in the pot and close the Crisping Lid.

2. Press Dehydrate, set the temperature to 135°F, and set the time to 12 hours. Select Start/Stop to begin.

3. When dehydrating is complete, remove the basket from the pot and transfer the jerky to an airtight container.

**Per serving** Calories: 46; Total fat: 0g; Saturated fat: 0g; Cholesterol: 0mg; Sodium: 6mg; Carbohydrates: 12g; Fiber: 1g; Protein: 1g

**PREP TIME**
5 MINUTES

**TOTAL COOK TIME**
12 HOURS

**DEHYDRATE**
12 HOURS

**ACCESSORIES**
COOK & CRISP™ BASKET, CRISPING LID

**DAIRY-FREE, GLUTEN-FREE, NUT-FREE, VEGAN**

**TIP:** Add a little zing to your watermelon jerky by sprinkling the watermelon with some sea salt and black pepper, paprika, cayenne pepper, or a squeeze of lime juice before placing it in the Ninja® Foodi.™

# Dried Mango

*I travel a lot for work, and I am always looking for healthy snacks at the airport. More often than not I reach for dried fruits and nuts. Unfortunately, prepackaged dried fruits can be packed with sugar and preservatives. These dried mangos are made from 100 percent real fruit with no added sugar, making them a smart snack choice.*

**½ mango, peeled, pitted, and cut into ⅜-inch slices**

1. Arrange the mango slices flat in a single layer in the Cook & Crisp Basket. Place in the pot and close the Crisping Lid.

2. Press Dehydrate, set the temperature to 135ºF, and set the time to 8 hours. Select Start/Stop to begin.

3. When dehydrating is complete, remove the basket from the pot and transfer the mango slices to an airtight container.

**Per serving** Calories: 67; Total fat: 0g; Saturated fat: 0g; Cholesterol: 0mg; Sodium: 2mg; Carbohydrates: 18g; Fiber: 2g; Protein: 1g

**PREP TIME**
5 MINUTES

**TOTAL COOK TIME**
8 HOURS

**DEHYDRATE**
8 HOURS

**ACCESSORIES**
COOK & CRISP™ BASKET, CRISPING LID

**DAIRY-FREE, GLUTEN-FREE, NUT-FREE, VEGAN**

**TIP:** Use the Dehydrate feature to turn a variety of fruits into tasty snacks. Try apples, bananas, pineapple, and strawberries. Cook time and prep instructions for these foods are listed in the Dehydrate chart (page 171).

# Beet Chips

*I'm always looking for ways to incorporate more vegetables into my diet. Dehydrated veggies are a great alternative to potato chips. They are cooked low and slow, so they get extra crispy. Step up your dehydrating game with salt and vinegar beet chips by soaking the beet slices in apple cider vinegar for 12 to 24 hours before dehydrating, then sprinkle lightly with salt once the beets are layered in the basket.*

**½ beet, peeled and cut into ⅛-inch slices**

1. Arrange the beet slices flat in a single layer in the Cook & Crisp Basket. Place in the pot and close the Crisping Lid.

2. Press Dehydrate, set the temperature to 135°F, and set the time to 8 hours. Select Start/Stop to begin.

3. When dehydrating is complete, remove the basket from the pot and transfer the beet chips to an airtight container.

**Per serving** Calories: 35; Total fat: 0g; Saturated fat: 0g; Cholesterol: 0mg; Sodium: 64mg; Carbohydrates: 8g; Fiber: 2g; Protein: 1g

**PREP TIME**
5 MINUTES

**TOTAL COOK TIME**
8 HOURS

**DEHYDRATE**
8 HOURS

**ACCESSORIES**
COOK & CRISP™ BASKET, CRISPING LID

**DAIRY-FREE, GLUTEN-FREE, NUT-FREE, VEGAN**

**TIP:** Use a mandoline to ensure that the beet is sliced evenly into consistent ⅛-inch slices.

# Maple Candied Bacon

*Bacon is trendy. It's everywhere: It's used as a garnish, infused into salt, and wrapped around roasts, and, believe it or not, you can even buy bacon-flavored toothpaste. Not only does the Ninja® Foodi™ make cooking bacon a breeze, but bacon, paired with maple syrup and brown sugar, is transformed into the perfect sweet and salty snack. Enjoy this candied bacon on its own or crumble it on top of soups, salads, and deviled eggs.*

½ cup maple syrup
¼ cup brown sugar

Nonstick cooking spray
1 pound (12 slices) thick-cut bacon

**PREP TIME**
5 MINUTES

**TOTAL COOK TIME**
40 MINUTES

**AIR CRISP**
40 MINUTES

**ACCESSORIES**
REVERSIBLE RACK, CRISPING LID

**DAIRY-FREE, GLUTEN-FREE, NUT-FREE**

**TIP:** Do you like a little spice? Turn this recipe into a Spicy Maple Candied Bacon by adding ½ teaspoon of cayenne pepper to the maple-syrup-sugar mixture in step 2.

1. Place the Reversible Rack in the pot. Close the Crisping Lid. Preheat the unit by selecting Air Crisp, setting the temperature to 400°F, and setting the time to 5 minutes.

2. Meanwhile, in a small mixing bowl, mix together the maple syrup and brown sugar.

3. Once the Ninja Foodi has preheated, carefully line the Reversible Rack with aluminum foil. Spray the foil with cooking spray.

4. Arrange 4 to 6 slices of bacon on the rack in a single layer. Brush them with the maple syrup mixture.

5. Close the Crisping Lid. Select Air Crisp and set the temperature to 400°F. Set the time to 10 minutes, then select Start/Stop to begin.

6. After 10 minutes, flip the bacon and brush with more maple syrup mixture. Close the Crisping Lid, select Air Crisp, set the temperature to 400°F, and set the time to 10 minutes. Select Start/Stop to begin.

7. Cooking is complete when your desired crispiness is reached. Remove the bacon from the Reversible Rack and transfer to a cooling rack for 10 minutes. Repeat steps 4 through 6 with the remaining bacon.

**Per serving (2 slices)** Calories: 451; Total fat: 34g; Saturated fat: 11g; Cholesterol: 51mg; Sodium: 634mg; Carbohydrates: 27g; Fiber: 0g; Protein: 9g

# Chili-Ranch Chicken Wings

**SERVES 4**

*When we created the Ninja® Foodi™, people loved making chicken wings. Crispy wings straight from the freezer also became a favorite in the Ninja Test Kitchen. This version is a tempting combination of spicy and cool that is sure to have you licking your fingers. Toss the wings in any sauce you want. I love using teriyaki or sweet chili sauce.*

½ cup water

½ cup hot pepper sauce

2 tablespoons unsalted butter, melted

1½ tablespoons apple cider vinegar

2 pounds frozen chicken wings

½ (1-ounce) envelope ranch salad dressing mix

½ teaspoon paprika

Nonstick cooking spray

**PREP TIME**
10 MINUTES

**TOTAL COOK TIME**
28 MINUTES

**APPROX. PRESSURE BUILD**
6 MINUTES

**PRESSURE COOK**
5 MINUTES

**PRESSURE RELEASE**
2 MINUTES

**AIR CRISP**
15 MINUTES

**ACCESSORIES**
COOK & CRISP™ BASKET, PRESSURE LID, CRISPING LID

**GLUTEN-FREE, NUT-FREE, UNDER 30 MINUTES**

1. Pour the water, hot pepper sauce, butter, and vinegar into the pot. Place the wings in the Cook & Crisp Basket and place the basket in the pot. Assemble the Pressure Lid, making sure the pressure release valve is in the Seal position.

2. Select Pressure and set to High. Set the time to 5 minutes. Select Start/Stop to begin.

3. When pressure cooking is complete, quick release the pressure by turning the pressure release valve to the Vent position. Carefully remove the lid when the unit has finished releasing pressure.

4. Sprinkle the chicken wings with the dressing mix and paprika. Coat with cooking spray.

5. Close the Crisping Lid. Select Air Crisp, set the temperature to 375ºF, and set the time to 15 minutes. Select Start/Stop to begin.

6. After 7 minutes, open the Crisping Lid, then lift the basket and shake the wings. Coat with cooking spray. Lower the basket back into the pot and close the lid to resume cooking until the wings reach your desired crispiness.

**TIP:** Using fresh wings instead of frozen? Follow the instructions in the Air Crisp chart on page 163.

**Per serving** Calories: 405; Total fat: 30g; Saturated fat: 10g; Cholesterol: 131mg; Sodium: 1782mg; Carbohydrates: 4g; Fiber: 0g; Protein: 28g

# Crispy Cheesy Arancini

**SERVES 6**

*I developed this recipe specifically for my little brother. A few months ago, I took him out to lunch at a local Italian joint, and we started the meal with fried rice croquettes. He loved them so much that we ordered seconds, and he hasn't stopped talking about them. There is something irresistible about the creamy, cheesy rice paired with the crispy, crunchy exterior that will keep you coming back for more.*

½ cup extra-virgin olive oil, plus 1 tablespoon

1 small yellow onion, diced

2 garlic cloves, minced

5 cups chicken broth

½ cup white wine

2 cups arborio rice

1½ cups grated Parmesan cheese, plus more for garnish

1 cup frozen peas

1 teaspoon sea salt

1 teaspoon freshly ground black pepper

2 cups fresh bread crumbs

2 large eggs

**PREP TIME**
15 MINUTES

**TOTAL COOK TIME**
45 MINUTES

**SEAR/SAUTÉ**
1 MINUTE

**APPROX. PRESSURE BUILD**
6 MINUTES

**PRESSURE COOK**
7 MINUTES

**PRESSURE RELEASE**
11 MINUTES

**AIR CRISP**
20 MINUTES

**ACCESSORIES**
COOK & CRISP™ BASKET, PRESSURE LID, CRISPING LID

**NUT-FREE**

**TIP:** For best results, let the risotto cool before step 8 or use leftover risotto from Lemon Risotto and Roasted Carrots (page 64) and skip steps 1 through 5.

1. Select Sear/Sauté and set to Medium High. Select Start/Stop to begin. Allow the pot to preheat for 5 minutes.

2. Add 1 tablespoon of oil and the onion to the preheated pot. Cook until soft and translucent, stirring occasionally. Add the garlic and cook for 1 minute.

3. Add the broth, wine, and rice to the pot; stir to incorporate. Assemble the Pressure Lid, making sure the pressure release valve is in the Seal position.

4. Select Pressure and set to High. Set the time to 7 minutes. Press Start/Stop to begin.

5. When pressure cooking is complete, allow pressure to naturally release for 10 minutes, then quick release any remaining pressure by turning the pressure release valve to the Vent position. Carefully remove the lid when the unit has finished releasing pressure.

6. Add the Parmesan cheese, frozen peas, salt, and pepper. Stir vigorously until the rice begins to thicken. Transfer the risotto to a large mixing bowl and let cool. ➤

7.  Meanwhile, clean the pot. In a medium mixing bowl, stir together the bread crumbs and the remaining ½ cup of olive oil. In a separate mixing bowl, lightly beat the eggs.

8.  Divide the risotto into 12 equal portions and form each one into a ball. Dip each risotto ball in the beaten eggs, then coat in the bread crumb mixture.

9.  Arrange half of the arancini in the Cook & Crisp™ Basket in a single layer.

10.  Close the Crisping Lid. Select Air Crisp, set the temperature to 400°F, and set the time to 10 minutes. Select Start/Stop to begin.

11.  Repeat steps 9 and 10 to cook the remaining arancini.

**Per serving** Calories: 769; Total fat: 32g; Saturated fat: 9g; Cholesterol: 98mg; Sodium: 1348mg; Carbohydrates: 91g; Fiber: 5g; Protein: 27g

# Buffalo Chicken Meatballs

*This recipe is not only a twist on your favorite football appetizer, but it also makes a whole platter of bite-size snacks. With buffalo sauce and ground chicken in the meatballs, every bite is filled with the buffalo chicken flavors we all love. Serve these as an appetizer on game day or turn them into a meal by serving them over a bed of zucchini noodles.*

1 pound ground chicken

1 carrot, minced

2 celery stalks, minced

¼ cup crumbled blue cheese

¼ cup buffalo sauce

¼ cup bread crumbs

1 egg

2 tablespoons extra-virgin olive oil

½ cup water

**PREP TIME**
10 MINUTES

**TOTAL COOK TIME**
40 MINUTES

**SEAR/SAUTÉ**
17 MINUTES

**APPROX. PRESSURE BUILD**
6 MINUTES

**PRESSURE COOK**
5 MINUTES

**PRESSURE RELEASE**
2 MINUTES

**AIR CRISP**
10 MINUTES

**ACCESSORIES**
COOK & CRISP™ BASKET, PRESSURE LID, CRISPING LID

**NUT-FREE**

1. Select Sear/Sauté and set to High. Select Start/Stop to begin. Allow the pot to preheat for 5 minutes.

2. Meanwhile, in a large mixing bowl, mix together the chicken, carrot, celery, blue cheese, buffalo sauce, bread crumbs, and egg. Shape the mixture into 1½-inch meatballs.

3. Pour the olive oil into the preheated pot. Working in batches, place the meatballs in the pot and sear on all sides until browned. When each batch finishes cooking, transfer to a plate.

4. Place the Cook & Crisp Basket in the pot. Add the water, then place all the meatballs in the basket.

5. Assemble the Pressure Lid, making sure the pressure release valve is in the Seal position. Select Pressure and set to High. Set the time to 5 minutes. Select Start/Stop to begin.

6. When pressure cooking is complete, quick release the pressure by turning the pressure release valve to the Vent position. Carefully remove the lid when the unit has finished releasing pressure. ➤

7. Close the Crisping Lid. Select Air Crisp, set the temperature to 360ºF, and set the time to 10 minutes. Select Start/Stop to begin.

8. After 5 minutes, open the lid, then lift the basket and shake the meatballs. Lower the basket back into the pot and close the lid to resume cooking until the meatballs achieve your desired crispiness.

**Per serving** Calories: 204; Total fat: 13g; Saturated fat: 4g; Cholesterol: 104mg; Sodium: 566mg; Carbohydrates: 5g; Fiber: 1g; Protein: 16g

# Loaded Smashed Potatoes

SERVES 4

*The best appetizers come in the form of mini mains. These potatoes don't stop at crispy, crunchy deliciousness, because they are topped with all of your favorite loaded baked potato add-ons. I love to fill these little bites with cheesy, bacon-y, creamy goodness. Want to add some spice with jalapeños? Go for it! Do you like to top your potatoes with some chili? Pile it on!*

**12 ounces baby Yukon gold potatoes**

**1 teaspoon extra-virgin olive oil**

**¼ cup sour cream**

**¼ cup shredded Cheddar cheese**

**2 slices bacon, cooked and crumbled**

**1 tablespoon chopped fresh chives**

**Sea salt**

**PREP TIME**
10 MINUTES

**TOTAL COOK TIME**
30 MINUTES

**AIR CRISP**
30 MINUTES

**ACCESSORIES**
COOK & CRISP™ BASKET, CRISPING LID

**GLUTEN-FREE, NUT-FREE, UNDER 30 MINUTES**

1. Place the Cook & Crisp Basket in the pot. Close the Crisping Lid. Preheat the unit by selecting Air Crisp, setting the temperature to 350ºF, and setting the time to 5 minutes. Press Start/Stop to begin.

2. Meanwhile, toss the potatoes with the oil until evenly coated.

3. Once the pot and basket are preheated, open the lid and add the potatoes to the basket. Close the lid, select Air Crisp, set the temperature to 350ºF, and set the time to 30 minutes. Press Start/Stop to begin.

4. After 15 minutes, open the lid, then lift the basket and shake the potatoes. Lower the basket back into the pot and close the lid to resume cooking.

5. After 15 minutes, check the potatoes for your desired crispiness. They should be fork tender.

6. Remove the potatoes from the basket. Use a large spoon to lightly crush the potatoes to split them. Top with the sour cream, cheese, bacon, and chives, and season with salt.

**Per serving** Calories: 154; Total fat: 8g; Saturated fat: 4g; Cholesterol: 19mg; Sodium: 152mg; Carbohydrates: 16g; Fiber: 1g; Protein: 5g

# Fried Dumplings

*Traditionally, dumplings are either steamed or panfried to perfection. In this recipe, I use Air Crisp to give each dumpling a delicious golden-brown, crunchy, crisp exterior. Gone are the days of soggy takeout, because once you try dumplings this way, you will never go back. Plus, you can freeze them before Air Crisping, so you can satisfy your dumpling craving whenever you want. Pop them in the Ninja® Foodi™ straight from the freezer.*

8 ounces ground pork

1 carrot, shredded

½ cup shredded Napa cabbage

1 large egg, beaten

1 garlic clove, minced

2 tablespoons reduced-sodium soy sauce

½ tablespoon sesame oil

½ tablespoon grated fresh ginger

½ teaspoon sea salt

½ teaspoon freshly ground black pepper

20 wonton wrappers

2 tablespoons vegetable oil

**PREP TIME**
20 MINUTES

**TOTAL COOK TIME**
12 MINUTES

**AIR CRISP**
12 MINUTES

**ACCESSORIES**
COOK & CRISP™ BASKET, CRISPING LID

**DAIRY-FREE, NUT-FREE, UNDER 30 MINUTES**

**TIP:** Can't find wonton or dumpling wrappers at the grocery store? You can use egg roll wrappers instead. You can also swap out the ground pork in this recipe for ground chicken or beef.

1. Place the Cook & Crisp Basket in the pot. Close the Crisping Lid. Preheat the unit by selecting Air Crisp, setting the temperature to 400°F, and setting the time to 5 minutes.

2. Meanwhile, in a large mixing bowl, combine the pork, carrot, cabbage, egg, garlic, soy sauce, sesame oil, ginger, salt, and pepper.

3. Place the wonton wrappers on a clean work surface and spoon 1 tablespoon of the pork mixture into the center of each wrapper. Gently rub the edges of the wrappers with water. Fold the dough over the filling to create a half-moon shape, pinching the edges to seal. Brush the dumplings with the vegetable oil.

4.  Place the dumplings in the Cook & Crisp™ Basket. Select Air Crisp, set the temperature to 400ºF, and set the time to 12 minutes. Select Start/Stop to begin.

5.  After 6 minutes, open the lid, then lift the basket and shake the dumplings. Lower the basket back into the pot and close the lid to resume cooking until the dumplings achieve your desired crispiness.

**Per serving** Calories: 186; Total fat: 11g; Saturated fat: 3g; Cholesterol: 49mg; Sodium: 424mg; Carbohydrates: 13g; Fiber: 1g; Protein: 8g

# Spinach-Artichoke Bites

**SERVES 8**

*Spinach and artichoke is a classic combination that is used in everything from breakfast quiches to dips, and even in ravioli fillings. It is served piping hot as often as it is served chilled. Here I use it as a creamy filling for mini phyllo dough bites that are crisp and flaky on the outside. You can easily adapt this recipe by simply switching up the filling. Try a goat cheese and fig filling, or a crab dip filling. Or change the game completely and use Nutella and bananas. You know you want to!*

¼ cup frozen chopped spinach

¼ cup finely chopped artichoke hearts

¼ cup cottage cheese

¼ cup feta cheese

2 tablespoons grated Parmesan cheese

1 large egg white

Zest of 1 lemon

1 teaspoon dried oregano

½ teaspoon sea salt

½ teaspoon freshly ground black pepper

4 (13-by-18-inch) sheets frozen phyllo dough, thawed

1 tablespoon extra-virgin olive oil

**PREP TIME**
20 MINUTES

**TOTAL COOK TIME**
24 MINUTES

**AIR CRISP**
24 MINUTES

**ACCESSORIES**
COOK & CRISP™ BASKET, CRISPING LID

**NUT-FREE, VEGETARIAN, UNDER 30 MINUTES**

**TIP:** If you have leftover filling, serve it with crackers or freeze it for later.

1. In a medium mixing bowl, combine the spinach, artichoke hearts, cottage cheese, feta cheese, Parmesan cheese, egg white, lemon zest, oregano, salt, and pepper.

2. Place the Cook & Crisp Basket in the pot. Close the Crisping Lid. Preheat the unit by selecting Air Crisp, setting the temperature to 375°F, and setting the time to 5 minutes. Press Start/Stop to begin.

3. Meanwhile, place 1 phyllo sheet on a clean work surface. Brush it all over with some of the olive oil. Place a second sheet of phyllo on top of the first and brush it with more oil. Continue layering to form a stack of 4 oiled sheets.

4. Working from the short side, cut the stack of phyllo sheets into 8 (2¼-inch-wide) strips. Cut the strips in half to form 16 (2¼-inch-wide) strips.

5.  Spoon about 1 tablespoon of filling onto 1 short end of each strip. Fold one corner over the filling to create a triangle; continue folding back and forth to the end of the strip, creating a triangle-shaped phyllo packet. Repeat until you have formed 16 phyllo bites.

6.  Open the Crisping Lid and arrange half of the phyllo bites in the basket in a single layer. Close the lid, select Air Crisp, set the temperature to 350°F, and set the time to 12 minutes. Press Start/Stop to begin.

7.  After 6 minutes, open the lid and flip the bites over. Lower the basket back into the pot and close the lid to resume cooking.

8.  After 6 minutes, check the packets for your desired crispiness. If done, remove the bites from the basket.

9.  Repeat steps 6, 7, and 8 with the remaining bites.

**Per serving** Calories: 75; Total fat: 4g; Saturated fat: 1g; Cholesterol: 5mg; Sodium: 310mg; Carbohydrates: 7g; Fiber: 1g; Protein: 3g

# Loaded Cauliflower Soup

**SERVES 8**

*This may be my best version of cauliflower soup yet, because the Ninja® Foodi™ makes quick work of building a flavorful soup. By sautéing the onion, garlic, and bacon with the Sear/Sauté feature, the flavor you are able to build is incredible. But the Ninja Foodi doesn't stop there. Top the soup with cheese and use the Crisping Lid to achieve a golden-brown and delicious bubbly cheese top. Once you have the technique down, the options are endless.*

5 slices bacon, chopped

1 onion, chopped

3 garlic cloves, minced

1 head cauliflower, trimmed into florets

4 cups chicken broth

1 cup whole milk

1 teaspoon sea salt

1 teaspoon freshly ground black pepper

1½ cups shredded Cheddar cheese

Sour cream, for serving (optional)

Chopped fresh chives, for serving (optional)

**PREP TIME**
15 MINUTES

**TOTAL COOK TIME**
29 MINUTES

**SEAR/SAUTÉ**
5 MINUTES

**APPROX. PRESSURE BUILD**
8 MINUTES

**PRESSURE COOK**
10 MINUTES

**PRESSURE RELEASE**
1 MINUTE

**BROIL**
5 MINUTES

**ACCESSORIES**
PRESSURE LID, CRISPING LID

**GLUTEN-FREE, NUT-FREE, UNDER 30 MINUTES**

1. Select Sear/Sauté and set to High. Select Start/Stop to begin. Allow the pot to preheat for 5 minutes.

2. Put the bacon, onion, and garlic in the preheated pot. Cook, stirring occasionally, for 5 minutes. Reserve some of the bacon for garnish.

3. Add the cauliflower and chicken broth to the pot. Assemble the Pressure Lid, making sure the pressure release valve is in the Seal position.

4. Select Pressure and set to High. Set the time to 10 minutes, then select Start/Stop to begin.

5. When pressure cooking is complete, quick release the pressure by moving the pressure release valve to the Vent position. Carefully remove the lid when the pressure has finished releasing.

6. Add the milk and mash until the soup reaches your desired consistency. Season with the salt and black pepper. Sprinkle the cheese evenly over the top of the soup.

7. Close the Crisping Lid. Select Broil and set the time to 5 minutes. Select Start/Stop to begin.

8. When cooking is complete, top with the reserved crispy bacon and serve immediately, with sour cream and chives (if using).

**Per serving** Calories: 253; Total fat: 17g; Saturated fat: 8g; Cholesterol: 41mg; Sodium: 774mg; Carbohydrates: 12g; Fiber: 2g; Protein: 13g

# 5

# Vegetarian Mains

Left: Mushroom and Gruyère Tarts, page 56

# Potato and Crispy Leek Soup

## SERVES 6

*The juxtaposition of a creamy soup base and crispy, crunchy leeks takes this version of potato and leek soup a step above any version you've ever had. I used to order a version of this soup for lunch on rainy afternoons while I was studying abroad in Auckland, New Zealand. Whether you are in a foreign land or at home on a rainy day, this soup is sure to be comforting.*

**2 tablespoons extra-virgin olive oil, divided**

**4 leeks, cleaned and thinly sliced, divided**

**4 garlic cloves, minced**

**5 Yukon gold potatoes, peeled and diced**

**3 thyme sprigs, stems removed**

**2 bay leaves**

**5 cups vegetable broth**

**¾ cup white wine**

**1½ teaspoons dried oregano**

**1 teaspoon sea salt**

**½ teaspoon freshly ground black pepper**

**1½ cups light cream**

**½ cup grated Cheddar cheese**

**PREP TIME**
15 MINUTES

**TOTAL COOK TIME**
31 MINUTES

**SEAR/SAUTÉ**
6 MINUTES

**APPROX. PRESSURE BUILD**
8 MINUTES

**PRESSURE COOK**
10 MINUTES

**PRESSURE RELEASE**
2 MINUTES

**BROIL**
5 MINUTES

**ACCESSORIES**
REVERSIBLE RACK, PRESSURE LID, CRISPING LID

**GLUTEN-FREE, NUT-FREE, VEGETARIAN**

**TIP:** I like a little texture in this soup, but if you prefer a thinner or smoother texture, transfer the soup to a high-speed blender in step 6 instead of mashing with a potato masher.

1. Select Sear/Sauté and set to Medium High. Select Start/Stop to begin. Allow the pot to preheat for 5 minutes.

2. Put 1 tablespoon of oil and three-quarters of the sliced leeks in the pot. Cook until soft, about 5 minutes. Add the garlic and cook for 1 minute more.

3. Add the potatoes, thyme, bay leaves, vegetable broth, white wine, oregano, salt, and black pepper to the pot. Assemble the Pressure Lid, making sure the pressure release valve is in the Seal position.

4. Select Pressure and set to High. Set the time to 10 minutes, then select Start/Stop to begin.

5. When pressure cooking is complete, quick release the pressure by moving the pressure release valve to the Vent position. Carefully remove the lid when the unit has finished releasing pressure.

6. Remove and discard the bay leaves. Add the cream and use a potato masher to mash the soup to your desired consistency. Evenly top with the cheese.

7. In a small bowl, toss the remaining sliced leeks with the remaining 1 tablespoon of oil. Place the Reversible Rack in the pot in the higher position. Place a sheet of aluminum foil on top of the rack and arrange the leeks on top.

8. Close the Crisping Lid. Select Broil and set the time to 5 minutes. Select Start/Stop to begin.

9. When cooking is complete, check to see if the leeks have reached your desired crispiness. Remove the rack from the pot and serve the crispy leeks over the soup.

**Per serving** Calories: 397; Total fat: 20g; Saturated fat: 10g; Cholesterol: 49mg; Sodium: 950mg; Carbohydrates: 47g; Fiber: 4g; Protein: 9g

# Chickpea, Spinach, and Sweet Potato Stew

*Pressure cookers make a stew that's as hearty, flavorful, and tender as if you had cooked it for hours on the stove. This vegan stew is great with any root vegetable that takes hours to tenderize on the stove; it goes from raw to melt-in-your-mouth in just minutes. Use this recipe as a base for other vegetarian and vegan stews: Just swap out the sweet potato for other root veggies and the chickpeas for whatever lentils or beans you have in the pantry.*

1 tablespoon extra-virgin olive oil

1 yellow onion, diced

4 garlic cloves, minced

4 sweet potatoes, peeled and diced

4 cups vegetable broth

1 (15-ounce) can fire-roasted diced tomatoes, undrained

2 (15-ounce) cans chickpeas, drained

1½ teaspoons ground cumin

1 teaspoon ground coriander

½ teaspoon paprika

½ teaspoon sea salt

½ teaspoon freshly ground black pepper

4 cups baby spinach

**PREP TIME**
15 MINUTES

**TOTAL COOK TIME**
23 MINUTES

**SEAR/SAUTÉ**
5 MINUTES

**APPROX. PRESSURE BUILD**
8 MINUTES

**PRESSURE COOK**
8 MINUTES

**PRESSURE RELEASE**
2 MINUTES

**ACCESSORIES**
PRESSURE LID

**DAIRY-FREE, GLUTEN-FREE, NUT-FREE, VEGAN, UNDER 30 MINUTES**

**TIP:** If you would prefer to assemble this recipe before you go into the office so there's a nice warm bowl of stew waiting for you when you get home, instead of using Pressure, select Slow Cook and set to Low for 6 to 7 hours.

1. Select Sear/Sauté and set to Medium High. Select Start/Stop to begin. Allow the pot to preheat for 5 minutes.

2. Combine the oil, onion, and garlic in the pot. Cook, stirring occasionally, for 5 minutes.

3. Add the sweet potatoes, vegetable broth, tomatoes, chickpeas, cumin, coriander, paprika, salt, and black pepper to the pot. Assemble the Pressure Lid, making sure the pressure release valve is in the Seal position.

4. Select Pressure and set to High. Set the time to 8 minutes, then select Start/Stop to begin.

5. When pressure cooking is complete, quick release the pressure by moving the pressure release valve to the Vent position. Carefully remove the lid when the unit has finished releasing pressure.

6. Add the spinach to the pot and stir until wilted. Serve.

**Per serving** Calories: 220; Total fat: 4g; Saturated fat: 0g; Cholesterol: 0mg; Sodium: 593mg; Carbohydrates: 42g; Fiber: 8g; Protein: 7g

# Mushroom and Gruyère Tarts

*These tarts may sound like a recipe for only the fanciest get-together, but they are super easy to make in a pinch for impromptu guests—and they're sure to impress. They're creamy on the inside, with flaky, buttery layers on the outside, and you can guarantee that everyone will be fighting over the last one.*

2 tablespoons extra-virgin olive oil, divided

1 small white onion, sliced

5 ounces shiitake mushrooms, sliced

¼ teaspoon sea salt

¼ teaspoon freshly ground black pepper

¼ cup dry white wine

1 sheet puff pastry, thawed

1 cup shredded Gruyère cheese

1 tablespoon thinly sliced fresh chives

**PREP TIME**
15 MINUTES

**TOTAL COOK TIME**
31 MINUTES

**SEAR/SAUTÉ**
7 MINUTES

**AIR CRISP**
24 MINUTES

**ACCESSORIES**
COOK & CRISP™ BASKET, CRISPING LID

**NUT-FREE, VEGETARIAN**

**TIP:** These tarts make for a tasty appetizer or a light meal. When served as a main, pair them with a mixed green salad dressed with mustard vinaigrette.

1. Select Sear/Sauté and set to High. Select Start/Stop to begin. Allow the pot to preheat for 5 minutes.

2. Combine 1 tablespoon of oil, the onion, and the mushrooms in the pot. Cook, stirring occasionally, for 5 minutes, or until the vegetables are browned and tender. Season with the salt and black pepper, then add the wine and cook until it has evaporated, about 2 minutes. Transfer the vegetables to a bowl and set aside.

3. Unfold the puff pastry and cut it into 4 squares. Using a fork, pierce the dough and brush both sides with the remaining 1 tablespoon of oil.

4. Evenly divide half the cheese among the puff pastry squares, leaving a ½-inch border around the edges. Divide the mushroom and onion mixture among the pastry squares, then divide the remaining cheese among them.

5. Place the Cook & Crisp Basket in the pot. Close the Crisping Lid. Preheat the unit by selecting Air Crisp, setting the temperature to 400°F, and setting the time to 5 minutes.

6. Once preheated, place 1 tart in the Cook & Crisp™ Basket.

7. Close the Crisping Lid. Select Air Crisp, set the temperature to 360°F, and set the time to 6 minutes. Select Start/Stop to begin.

8. After 6 minutes, check for your desired browning. Remove the tart from the basket and transfer to a plate.

9. Repeat steps 6 through 8 with the remaining tarts.

10. Serve garnished with the chives.

**Per serving** Calories: 550; Total fat: 39g; Saturated fat: 12g; Cholesterol: 30mg; Sodium: 394mg; Carbohydrates: 34g; Fiber: 2g; Protein: 15g

# Stuffed Portobello Mushrooms

*Whenever I am looking for a quick and easy last-minute dinner, stuffed veggies are my go-to. Mushrooms and peppers work particularly well because they are already hollow. Stuff them with your favorite grain, more veggies, and simple seasoning, and—voilà!— dinner is ready. This recipe is a technique you can use over and over when making dinner in the Ninja® Foodi.™ Just swap out the ingredients below for what you already have. And don't forget the cheese!*

4 large portobello mushrooms, stems and gills removed

2 tablespoons extra-virgin olive oil

½ cup cooked quinoa

1 tomato, seeded and diced

1 bell pepper, seeded and diced

¼ cup Kalamata olives, pitted and chopped

½ cup crumbled feta cheese

Juice of 1 lemon

½ teaspoon sea salt

½ teaspoon freshly ground black pepper

Minced fresh parsley, for garnish

**PREP TIME**
15 MINUTES

**TOTAL COOK TIME**
28 MINUTES

**AIR CRISP**
28 MINUTES

**ACCESSORIES**
COOK & CRISP™ BASKET, CRISPING LID

**GLUTEN-FREE, NUT-FREE, VEGETARIAN, UNDER 30 MINUTES**

1. Place the Cook & Crisp Basket in the pot. Close the Crisping Lid. Preheat the unit by selecting Air Crisp, setting the temperature to 375ºF, and setting the time to 5 minutes. Press Start/Stop to begin.

2. Coat the mushrooms with the oil. Open the Crisping Lid and arrange the mushrooms, open-side up, in a single layer in the preheated Cook & Crisp Basket.

3. Close the Crisping Lid. Select Air Crisp, set the temperature to 375ºF, and set the time to 20 minutes. Select Start/Stop to begin.

4. In a medium mixing bowl, combine the quinoa, tomato, bell pepper, olives, feta cheese, lemon juice, salt, and black pepper.

5. Open the Crisping Lid and spoon the quinoa mixture evenly into the 4 mushrooms. Close the lid. Select Air Crisp, set the temperature to 350ºF, and set the time to 8 minutes. Press Start/Stop to begin.

6. Garnish with fresh parsley and serve immediately.

**Per serving** Calories: 228; Total fat: 12g; Saturated fat: 3g; Cholesterol: 21mg; Sodium: 604mg; Carbohydrates: 24g; Fiber: 4g; Protein: 8g

# Eggplant Parmesan and Spaghetti

**SERVES 4**

*When I got to take home the Ninja® Foodi™ for the first time, I was tasked with testing recipes and filming them to teach our team all about how to use this kitchen revolution! One of the first recipes I made was a chicken Parmesan, and the moment I opened the Crisping Lid and saw the crispy breading and golden-brown cheese, I knew I had to develop a version of eggplant Parmesan. This recipe was inspired by my mom, not only because it is her favorite but also because, growing up, I never understood why someone would order a veggie dish instead of pasta. Here, you don't have to choose!*

1 pound spaghetti

4 cups water, plus 2 tablespoons

2 teaspoons sea salt, divided

1 cup all-purpose flour

2 eggs

1 cup seasoned bread crumbs

½ cup grated Parmesan cheese, plus more for garnish

1 eggplant, peeled and sliced into ½-inch-thick rounds

1 (24-ounce) jar marinara sauce, divided

2 tablespoons extra-virgin olive oil

1 cup shredded mozzarella cheese

Minced fresh parsley, for garnish

**PREP TIME**
15 MINUTES

**TOTAL COOK TIME**
30 MINUTES

**APPROX. PRESSURE BUILD**
8 MINUTES

**PRESSURE COOK**
2 MINUTES

**PRESSURE RELEASE**
2 MINUTES

**AIR CRISP**
15 MINUTES

**BROIL**
3 MINUTES

**ACCESSORIES**
REVERSIBLE RACK, PRESSURE LID, CRISPING LID

**NUT-FREE, VEGETARIAN, UNDER 30 MINUTES, 360 MEAL**

**TIP:** If you are serving more than four people, use the remaining eggplant to make additional cutlets. If not, bread the remaining eggplant slices and store them in the freezer for a quick meal later in the week.

1. Break the spaghetti in half. Put it in the pot and add 4 cups of water and 1 teaspoon of salt. Assemble the Pressure Lid, making sure the pressure release valve is in the Seal position.

2. Select Pressure and set to High. Set the time to 2 minutes, then select Start/Stop to begin.

3. While the pasta is cooking, stir together the flour and remaining 1 teaspoon of salt in a shallow bowl. In another shallow bowl, whisk together the eggs and remaining 2 tablespoons of water. In a third shallow bowl, combine the bread crumbs and Parmesan cheese.

4. Working one at a time, coat each of 4 eggplant slices in the flour. Tap off any excess flour, then dip the eggplant in the egg wash. Transfer the eggplant to the bread crumbs, tossing well to evenly coat. Set aside. (See the Tip for what to do with the remaining eggplant slices.)

5. When pressure cooking the spaghetti is complete, quick release the pressure by moving the pressure release valve to the Vent position. Carefully remove the lid when the unit has finished releasing pressure.

6. Pour all but ¼ cup of the marinara sauce over the cooked pasta.

7. Place the Reversible Rack inside the pot over the pasta, making sure the rack is in the higher position. Place the breaded eggplant on the rack and brush lightly with the oil.

8. Close the Crisping Lid. Select Air Crisp, set the temperature to 350°F, and set the time to 15 minutes. Press Start/Stop to begin.

9. When cooking is complete, spread the remaining ¼ cup of marinara sauce on top of the eggplant. Top with the mozzarella cheese.

10. Close the Crisping Lid. Select Broil and set the time to 3 minutes. Select Start/Stop to begin.

11. When cooking is complete, garnish with fresh parsley and serve.

**Per serving** Calories: 972; Total fat: 23g; Saturated fat: 8g; Cholesterol: 138mg; Sodium: 1209mg; Carbohydrates: 150g; Fiber: 15g; Protein: 39g

# Veggie Shepherd's Pie

**SERVES 6**

*Sometimes I crave a meal that is packed full of delicious veggies—and this recipe delivers just that. In place of lamb or beef, vegetables are cooked in a decadent gravy and then covered with a layer of creamy mashed potatoes. Each step of this recipe builds flavor along the way. By braising the veggies, cooking the potatoes, and crisping the top to golden-brown perfection, you won't miss the meat one bit.*

1 tablespoon extra-virgin olive oil

1 onion, diced

16 ounces cremini mushrooms, sliced

6 carrots, diced

2 garlic cloves, minced

2 tablespoons tomato paste

2 cups vegetable broth

1 teaspoon dried thyme

¼ teaspoon dried rosemary

1 teaspoon sea salt

2 cups frozen peas

2 cups mashed potatoes

**PREP TIME**
10 MINUTES

**TOTAL COOK TIME**
22 MINUTES

**SEAR/SAUTÉ**
6 MINUTES

**APPROX. PRESSURE BUILD**
6 MINUTES

**PRESSURE COOK**
3 MINUTES

**PRESSURE RELEASE**
2 MINUTES

**BROIL**
5 MINUTES

**ACCESSORIES**
PRESSURE LID, CRISPING LID

**GLUTEN-FREE, NUT-FREE, VEGETARIAN, UNDER 30 MINUTES**

1. Select Sear/Sauté and set to High. Select Start/Stop to begin. Allow the pot to preheat for 5 minutes.

2. Once preheated, add the oil, onion, mushrooms, and carrots. Sauté until the mushrooms have released their liquid and the onion is translucent, about 5 minutes. Add the garlic and tomato paste and sauté for 1 minute more.

3. Add the vegetable broth and season with the thyme, rosemary, and salt. Assemble the Pressure Lid, making sure the pressure release valve is in the Seal position.

4. Select Pressure and set to High. Set the time to 3 minutes, then select Start/Stop to begin. When pressure cooking is complete, quick release the pressure by moving the pressure release valve to the Vent position. Carefully remove the lid when the pressure has finished releasing.

**TIP:** If you don't have leftover mashed potatoes on hand, you can easily whip up a batch in the Ninja® Foodi.™ Follow the chart on page 162 for pressure cooking potatoes for mashed potatoes. If the filling is thin after pressure cooking, stir in 1 to 2 tablespoons of the flour of your choice (gluten-free, all-purpose, etc.) before adding the peas.

5. Stir in the frozen peas, then spread the mixture in an even layer in the bottom of the pot. Spread the mashed potatoes evenly over the mixture. If desired, drag a fork over the potatoes to create a decorative topping.

6. Close the Crisping Lid. Select Broil and set the time to 5 minutes. Select Start/Stop to begin.

7. When cooking is complete, allow the shepherd's pie to rest for 10 minutes before serving.

**Per serving** Calories: 264; Total fat: 3g; Saturated fat: 0g; Cholesterol: 0mg; Sodium: 731mg; Carbohydrates: 53g; Fiber: 7g; Protein: 9g

# Lemon Risotto and Roasted Carrots

**SERVES 4**

*Risotto is notorious for being a dish that takes a long time and a lot of work. To make it the traditional way would require you to stand over a pot on the stove, stirring until it reaches the perfect consistency. With this recipe, you just pop in the ingredients and let the Ninja® Foodi™ do the work.*

2 tablespoons extra-virgin olive oil, divided

1 garlic clove, minced

5 cups vegetable broth

¼ cup freshly squeezed lemon juice

1 teaspoon grated lemon zest

2 cups arborio rice

2 teaspoons sea salt, divided

4 carrots, cut ¾ inch thick on the diagonal

1 teaspoon freshly ground black pepper

2 tablespoons unsalted butter

1½ cups grated Parmesan cheese, plus more for garnish

**PREP TIME**
10 MINUTES

**TOTAL COOK TIME**
34 MINUTES

**SEAR/SAUTÉ**
1 MINUTE

**APPROX. PRESSURE BUILD**
6 MINUTES

**PRESSURE COOK**
7 MINUTES

**PRESSURE RELEASE**
12 MINUTES

**BROIL**
8 MINUTES

**ACCESSORIES**
REVERSIBLE RACK, PRESSURE LID, CRISPING LID

**GLUTEN-FREE, NUT-FREE, VEGETARIAN, 360 MEAL**

**TIP:** Use this recipe as a formula to make endless variations of risotto. Try swapping out the lemon juice and zest from the base and instead sauté an onion with the garlic. Then play with the toppings. You can use other vegetables like mushrooms and Brussels sprouts. If you eat meat, try shrimp or chicken.

1. Select Sear/Sauté and set to Medium High. Select Start/Stop to begin. Allow the pot to preheat for 5 minutes.

2. Add 1 tablespoon of oil and the garlic to the preheated pot and cook until fragrant, about 1 minute. Add the broth, lemon juice, lemon zest, and rice to the pot. Season with 1 teaspoon of salt and stir to combine.

3. Assemble the Pressure Lid, making sure the pressure release valve is in the Seal position. Select Pressure and set to High. Set the time to 7 minutes, then select Start/Stop to begin.

4. While the rice is cooking, in a medium mixing bowl, toss together the carrots with the remaining 1 tablespoon of oil, the remaining 1 teaspoon of salt, and the black pepper.

5. When pressure cooking is complete, allow the pressure to naturally release for 10 minutes, then quick release any remaining pressure by moving the pressure release valve to the Vent position. Carefully remove the lid when the unit has finished releasing pressure.

6.  Stir the butter into the rice until evenly incorporated. Place the Reversible Rack inside the pot over the risotto, making sure the rack is in the higher position. Place the carrots on the rack.

7.  Close the Crisping Lid. Select Broil and set the time to 8 minutes. Select Start/Stop to begin.

8.  When cooking is complete, remove the rack from the pot. Stir the Parmesan cheese into the risotto. Top with the roasted carrots and garnish with additional Parmesan. Serve immediately.

**Per serving** Calories: 674; Total fat: 24g; Saturated fat: 11g; Cholesterol: 48mg; Sodium: 2468mg; Carbohydrates: 92g; Fiber: 5g; Protein: 22g

# Crispy Tofu with Roasted Sweet Potatoes and Rice

**SERVES 4**

*Most foods are made exponentially tastier when fried. I feel that this is especially true for tofu. I steer clear of these spongy little cubes unless they have a crispy, crunchy exterior. Since deep-frying tofu is not a feasible way to prepare dinner during the week, this recipe uses the Crisping Lid to re-create the crispy crunch I crave. Plus, this recipe is for a full meal, so you get rice and veggies, too.*

1 cup brown rice, rinsed

¾ cup water

1 sweet potato, peeled and diced

2 tablespoons extra-virgin olive oil, divided

1 teaspoon sea salt

1 teaspoon freshly ground black pepper

1 (15-ounce) block organic extra-firm tofu, drained and sliced into ½-inch cubes

1 tablespoon soy sauce

2 teaspoons cornstarch

1. Place the rice and water in the pot and stir to combine. Assemble the Pressure Lid, making sure the pressure release valve is in the Seal position. Select Pressure and set to High. Set the time to 2 minutes, then select Start/Stop to begin.

2. While the rice is cooking, in a small mixing bowl, toss the sweet potato in 1 tablespoon of olive oil and season with the salt and black pepper.

3. Ensure that the tofu is well-drained and all excess water is removed. In a medium mixing bowl, whisk together the remaining 1 tablespoon of olive oil and the soy sauce. Toss the tofu cubes in the soy sauce mixture, then add the cornstarch and toss until evenly coated.

4. When pressure cooking the rice is complete, quick release the pressure by moving the pressure release valve to the Vent position. Carefully remove the lid when the pressure has finished releasing.

**PREP TIME**
10 MINUTES

**TOTAL COOK TIME**
30 MINUTES

**APPROX. PRESSURE BUILD**
6 MINUTES

**PRESSURE COOK**
2 MINUTES

**PRESSURE RELEASE**
2 MINUTES

**AIR CRISP**
20 MINUTES

**ACCESSORIES**
REVERSIBLE RACK, PRESSURE LID, CRISPING LID

**DAIRY-FREE, NUT-FREE, VEGAN, UNDER 30 MINUTES, 360 MEAL**

**TIP:** This recipe makes a great lunch bowl. Serve the rice on the bottom and top with whatever else you have on hand—chopped peanuts, fresh kale, even diced mango. Make a batch on Sunday and enjoy it throughout the week.

5. Place the Reversible Rack in the pot in the higher position and line with aluminum foil. Arrange the sweet potatoes and tofu on the rack.

6. Close the Crisping Lid. Select Air Crisp, set the temperature to 400ºF, and set the time to 20 minutes. Select Start/Stop to begin. Use tongs to flip the sweet potatoes and tofu after 10 minutes.

7. When cooking is complete, check for your desired crispiness and serve.

---

**Per serving** Calories: 328; Total fat: 10g; Saturated fat: 2g; Cholesterol: 0mg; Sodium: 919mg; Carbohydrates: 47g; Fiber: 3g; Protein: 12g

# Zucchini Boats with Quinoa Stuffing

SERVES 4

*Zucchini boats are as delicious as they are beautiful. This Instagram-worthy dish can be filled based on any taste. Go Italian with tomatoes and cheese, Mediterranean with olives and feta, or Tex-Mex with black beans and corn—you really can't go wrong. This version has been on repeat in our house, and I think it will be in yours, too.*

2 small zucchini

½ cup cooked quinoa

½ cup canned cannellini beans, drained and rinsed

½ cup quartered cherry tomatoes

½ cup chopped almonds

½ cup grated Parmesan cheese, divided

2 tablespoons extra-virgin olive oil, divided

½ teaspoon sea salt

½ teaspoon freshly ground black pepper

**PREP TIME**
15 MINUTES

**TOTAL COOK TIME**
20 MINUTES

**AIR CRISP**
15 MINUTES

**BROIL**
5 MINUTES

**ACCESSORIES**
COOK & CRISP™ BASKET, CRISPING LID

**GLUTEN-FREE, VEGETARIAN, UNDER 30 MINUTES**

**TIP:** The Ninja® Foodi™ makes quick work of cooking grains. I like to make a batch of quinoa or rice and then use it throughout the week to add bulk to recipes like this one. If you don't have your quinoa premade, then follow the chart on page 159 to make quinoa for this recipe.

1. Halve each zucchini, then cut in half lengthwise and scoop out the inside, leaving a ½-inch-thick shell. Roughly chop the pulp.

2. In a large mixing bowl, combine the zucchini pulp, quinoa, cannellini beans, tomatoes, almonds, ¼ cup of Parmesan cheese, 1 tablespoon of olive oil, the salt, and the black pepper.

3. Place the Cook & Crisp Basket in the pot. Close the Crisping Lid. Preheat the unit by selecting Air Crisp, setting the temperature to 400ºF, and setting the time to 5 minutes.

4. Spoon the zucchini mixture into the zucchini shells and arrange the zucchini boats in a single layer in the preheated Cook & Crisp Basket.

5. Close the Crisping Lid. Select Air Crisp, set the temperature to 400ºF, and set the time to 15 minutes. Select Start/Stop to begin.

6. After 15 minutes, sprinkle the zucchini boats evenly with the remaining ¼ cup of Parmesan cheese and remaining 1 tablespoon of olive oil.

7. Close the Crisping Lid. Select Broil and set the time to 5 minutes. Select Start/Stop to begin.

8. When cooking is complete, check for your desired crispiness and serve.

**Per serving** Calories: 241; Total fat: 17g; Saturated fat: 4g; Cholesterol: 11mg; Sodium: 568mg; Carbohydrates: 15g; Fiber: 4g; Protein: 10g

# Creamy Polenta and Mushrooms

*Polenta, or grits, is really just a fancy word for ground cornmeal. It can be served a multi-tude of ways, including hot and creamy, baked, fried, or grilled. The trick to the perfect polenta, however, is to cook it for a long time and infuse it with flavor—otherwise you will be left with boring, bland mush. The Ninja® Foodi™ makes quick work of achieving the perfect polenta, cooked in broth to ensure that it is packed with flavor.*

**4 cups vegetable broth, divided**

**1 cup grits or coarse-ground cornmeal**

**2½ teaspoons sea salt, divided**

**1 cup shiitake mushrooms, sliced**

**1 teaspoon extra-virgin olive oil**

**½ teaspoon freshly ground black pepper**

**¼ cup grated Parmesan cheese**

**2 tablespoons chopped fresh sage, for garnish**

**PREP TIME**
10 MINUTES

**TOTAL COOK TIME**
30 MINUTES

**APPROX. PRESSURE BUILD**
6 MINUTES

**PRESSURE COOK**
4 MINUTES

**PRESSURE RELEASE**
12 MINUTES

**BROIL**
8 MINUTES

**ACCESSORIES**
REVERSIBLE RACK, PRESSURE LID, CRISPING LID

**GLUTEN-FREE, NUT-FREE, VEGETARIAN, UNDER 30 MINUTES, 360 MEAL**

**TIP:** It is important to use traditional grits or course-ground cornmeal in this recipe, and not instant polenta. If you want to sneak in even more veggies, try adding shredded Brussels sprouts in with the mushrooms.

1. Pour ½ cup of vegetable broth into the pot. Place the grits, 2 teaspoons of salt, and the remaining 3½ cups of broth into the Multi-Purpose Pan or an 8-inch baking pan. Stir to combine.

2. Place the pan onto the Reversible Rack, making sure the rack is in the lower position. Place the rack with the pan in the pot. Assemble the Pressure Lid, making sure the pressure release valve is in the Seal position.

3. Select Pressure and set to High. Set the time to 4 minutes, then select Start/Stop to begin.

4. While the grits are cooking, in a medium mixing bowl, toss the sliced mushrooms with the olive oil, black pepper, and remaining ½ teaspoon of salt. Coat thoroughly and set aside.

5. When pressure cooking the grits is complete, allow the pressure to naturally release for 10 minutes, then quick release any remaining pressure by moving the pressure release valve to the Vent position. Carefully remove the lid when the pressure has finished releasing.

6. Stir the Parmesan cheese into the grits until completely melted. Lay the mushrooms on top of the grits and close the Crisping Lid. Select Broil and set the time to 8 minutes. Select Start/Stop to begin.

7. When cooking is complete, garnish with the sage and serve.

**Per serving** Calories: 197; Total fat: 5g; Saturated fat: 2g; Cholesterol: 6mg; Sodium: 2102mg; Carbohydrates: 31g; Fiber: 4g; Protein: 7g

# 6

# Fish & Seafood Mains

Left: Crispy Fish Tacos, page 88

# Bang Bang Shrimp

## SERVES 4

*I'm not sure who named bang bang sauce or where the original version was developed, but I do know that it is delicious and the perfect complement to anything fried. This chili mayo–style sauce paired with Air Crisped shrimp checks all of the boxes: sweet and spicy, crispy and creamy. I make the recipe a full meal by pairing it with rice, but if you are looking for the perfect appetizer, you can make the shrimp on its own.*

**1 cup long-grain white rice**

**1 cup water**

**16 ounces frozen popcorn shrimp**

**½ cup mayonnaise**

**¼ cup sweet chili sauce**

**½ teaspoon Sriracha**

**2 tablespoons sliced scallions, for garnish**

**PREP TIME**
5 MINUTES

**TOTAL COOK TIME**
21 MINUTES

**APPROX. PRESSURE BUILD**
8 MINUTES

**PRESSURE COOK**
2 MINUTES

**PRESSURE RELEASE**
2 MINUTES

**AIR CRISP**
9 MINUTES

**ACCESSORIES**
REVERSIBLE RACK, PRESSURE LID, CRISPING LID

**GLUTEN-FREE, NUT-FREE, UNDER 30 MINUTES**

1. Put the rice and water in the pot and stir to combine. Assemble the Pressure Lid, making sure the pressure release valve is in the Seal position. Select Pressure and set to High. Set the time to 2 minutes, then select Start/Stop to begin.

2. When pressure cooking is complete, quick release the pressure by moving the pressure release valve to the Vent position. Carefully remove the lid when the pressure has finished releasing.

3. Place the Reversible Rack inside the pot over the rice, making sure the rack is in the higher position. Place the shrimp on the rack.

4. Close the Crisping Lid. Select Air Crisp, set the temperature to 390ºF, and set the time to 9 minutes. Select Start/Stop to begin.

5. Meanwhile, in a medium mixing bowl, stir together the mayonnaise, sweet chili sauce, and Sriracha to create the sauce.

**TIP:** Use this recipe to make bang bang chicken: Simply swap out the shrimp for boneless, skinless chicken chopped into 1-inch pieces. Cook for the same amount of time as the shrimp.

6.  After 5 minutes of Air Crisping time, use tongs to flip the shrimp. Close the lid to resume cooking.

7.  After cooking is complete, check for desired crispiness and remove the rack from the pot. Toss the shrimp in the sauce to coat evenly. Plate the rice and shrimp, garnish with the scallions, and serve.

**Per serving** Calories: 403; Total fat: 12g; Saturated fat: 2g; Cholesterol: 178mg; Sodium: 690mg; Carbohydrates: 48g; Fiber: 1g; Protein: 26g

# Chile-Lime Salmon with Broccoli and Brown Rice

**SERVES 4**

*For this recipe, I use frozen salmon fillets, which can be found year-round in the grocery store no matter where you are, and which are much easier to work with in the Ninja® Foodi™ than fresh salmon. A bright chile-lime sauce packs a ton of flavor into this recipe. The sauce is so addictive, you may want to double the recipe so you can drizzle it on the rice and broccoli, too.*

1 cup brown rice, rinsed

¾ cup water

4 (4-ounce) frozen skinless salmon fillets

1 small head broccoli, trimmed into florets

3 tablespoons extra-virgin olive oil, divided

1 teaspoon sea salt

1 teaspoon freshly ground black pepper

Juice of 2 limes

2 tablespoons honey

1 teaspoon paprika

4 garlic cloves, minced

2 jalapeño peppers, seeded and diced

2 tablespoons chopped fresh parsley

**PREP TIME**
10 MINUTES

**TOTAL COOK TIME**
19 MINUTES

**APPROX. PRESSURE BUILD**
8 MINUTES

**PRESSURE COOK**
2 MINUTES

**PRESSURE RELEASE**
2 MINUTES

**BROIL**
7 MINUTES

**ACCESSORIES**
REVERSIBLE RACK, PRESSURE LID, CRISPING LID

DAIRY-FREE, GLUTEN-FREE, NUT-FREE, UNDER 30 MINUTES, 360 MEAL

**TIP:** If you prefer to use fresh salmon in place of the frozen, simply place it on the rack in step 6 with the broccoli and Roast at 350°F for 12 minutes. This will ensure that your fish is not overcooked.

1. Put the rice and water in the pot and stir to combine. Place the Reversible Rack in the pot in the higher position. Place the salmon fillets on the rack.

2. Assemble the Pressure Lid, making sure the pressure release valve is in the Seal position. Select Pressure and set to High. Set the time to 2 minutes, then select Start/Stop to begin.

3. While the salmon and rice are cooking, in a medium bowl, toss the broccoli in 1 tablespoon of olive oil and season with the salt and black pepper. In a small bowl, mix together the remaining 2 tablespoons of oil, the lime juice, honey, paprika, garlic, jalapeño, and parsley.

4. When pressure cooking the rice and salmon is complete, quick release the pressure by moving the pressure release valve to the Vent position. Carefully remove the lid when the pressure has finished releasing.

5. Gently pat the salmon dry with a paper towel, then coat the fish with the jalapeño mixture, reserving some of the sauce for garnish.

6. Arrange the broccoli around the salmon. Close the Crisping Lid. Select Broil and set the time to 7 minutes. Select Start/ Stop to begin.

7. When cooking is complete, remove the salmon from the rack and serve it with the broccoli and rice. Garnish with the fresh parsley and the remaining sauce, as desired.

**Per serving** Calories: 475; Total fat: 19g; Saturated fat: 3g; Cholesterol: 62mg; Sodium: 648mg; Carbohydrates: 49g; Fiber: 3g; Protein: 27g

# Garlic Butter Salmon with Green Beans

SERVES 4

*In my opinion, butter makes everything better, but what makes butter better? Garlic. Garlic butter–smothered salmon is a given. It's delicious. But what makes this recipe extra special, beyond the garlicky, buttery deliciousness, is that it is a full meal. The quinoa is cooked to fluffy perfection, while the salmon is perfectly flaky and the green beans are charred and crispy.*

1 cup quinoa, rinsed

1½ cups water

4 (4-ounce) frozen skinless salmon fillets

8 ounces green beans

1 tablespoon extra-virgin olive oil

1 teaspoon sea salt, divided

1 teaspoon freshly ground black pepper, divided

4 tablespoons (½ stick) unsalted butter, melted

½ tablespoon brown sugar

½ tablespoon freshly squeezed lemon juice

2 garlic cloves, minced

½ teaspoon dried thyme

½ teaspoon dried rosemary

**PREP TIME**
10 MINUTES

**TOTAL COOK TIME**
19 MINUTES

**APPROX. PRESSURE BUILD**
8 MINUTES

**PRESSURE COOK**
2 MINUTES

**PRESSURE RELEASE**
2 MINUTES

**BROIL**
7 MINUTES

**ACCESSORIES**
REVERSIBLE RACK, PRESSURE LID, CRISPING LID

**GLUTEN-FREE, NUT-FREE, UNDER 30 MINUTES, 360 MEAL**

1. Put the quinoa and water in the pot and stir to combine. Place the Reversible Rack in the pot in the higher position.

2. Place the salmon fillets on the rack. Assemble the Pressure Lid, making sure the pressure release valve is in the Seal position.

3. Select Pressure and set to High. Set the time to 2 minutes, then select Start/Stop to begin.

4. While the salmon and rice are cooking, in a medium bowl, toss the green beans with the olive oil, ½ teaspoon of salt, and ½ teaspoon of black pepper. In a small bowl, mix together the remaining ½ teaspoon each of salt and black pepper, the butter, brown sugar, lemon juice, garlic, thyme, and rosemary.

5. When pressure cooking the rice and salmon is complete, quick release the pressure by moving the pressure release valve to the Vent position. Carefully remove the lid when the pressure has finished releasing.

6. Gently pat the salmon dry with a paper towel, then coat with the garlic butter sauce.

7. Arrange the green beans around the salmon. Close the Crisping Lid. Select Broil and set the time to 7 minutes, then select Start/Stop to begin.

8. When cooking is complete, remove the salmon from the rack and serve with the green beans and rice.

**Per serving** Calories: 471; Total fat: 24g; Saturated fat: 9g; Cholesterol: 92mg; Sodium: 638mg; Carbohydrates: 33g; Fiber: 5g; Protein: 29g

# Cod over Couscous

*Keeping a few variations of pasta and grains in the pantry means you will have the base for an endless number of meals at your fingertips. This light, Mediterranean-inspired dish is the ideal weeknight meal. Quick and simple, it is perfect for those who are intimidated by the idea of cooking fish at home. With minimal prep or oversight you can create expertly cooked fish and fluffy couscous.*

**1 tablespoon extra-virgin olive oil**

**1 red bell pepper, diced**

**1 yellow bell pepper, diced**

**2 cups tricolor Israeli or pearl couscous**

**2½ cups chicken broth**

**1 cup panko bread crumbs**

**4 tablespoons (½ stick) unsalted butter, melted**

**¼ cup minced fresh parsley**

**Juice of 1 lemon**

**1 teaspoon grated lemon zest**

**1 teaspoon sea salt**

**4 (5- to 6-ounce) cod fillets**

**PREP TIME**
10 MINUTES

**TOTAL COOK TIME**
27–29 MINUTES

**APPROX. PRESSURE BUILD**
8 MINUTES

**PRESSURE COOK**
6 MINUTES

**PRESSURE RELEASE**
1 MINUTE

**AIR CRISP**
12–14 MINUTES

**ACCESSORIES**
REVERSIBLE RACK, PRESSURE LID, CRISPING LID

**NUT-FREE, UNDER 30 MINUTES, 360 MEAL**

1. Select Sear/Sauté and set to Medium High. Select Start/Stop to begin. Allow the pot to preheat for 5 minutes.

2. Combine the oil, red and yellow bell peppers, and couscous in the preheated pot and cook for 1 minute. Stir in the chicken broth.

3. Assemble the Pressure Lid, making sure the pressure release valve is in the Seal position. Select Pressure and set to High. Set the time to 6 minutes, then select Start/Stop to begin.

4. Meanwhile, in a small mixing bowl, stir together the panko bread crumbs, butter, parsley, lemon juice, lemon zest, and salt. Press the panko mixture evenly on top of each cod fillet.

5. When pressure cooking the couscous is complete, quick release the pressure by moving the pressure release valve to the Vent position. Carefully remove the lid when the pressure has finished releasing.

6. Place the Reversible Rack in the pot over the couscous; making sure it is in the higher position. Place the cod fillets on the rack.

7. Close the Crisping Lid. Select Air Crisp, set the temperature to 350ºF, and set the time to 12 minutes. Select Start/Stop to begin. Check the cod and cook for up to an additional 2 minutes if necessary. Cooking is complete when the internal temperature of the fillets reaches 145ºF.

**Per serving** Calories: 751; Total fat: 20g; Saturated fat: 9g; Cholesterol: 95mg; Sodium: 1084mg; Carbohydrates: 96g; Fiber: 7g; Protein: 44g

# Corn Chowder with Spicy Shrimp

**SERVES 4**

*Corn chowder is a luscious, creamy soup bursting with the sweetness of corn. Here, the brightness of the corn contrasts with the smokiness of the spicy shrimp and crispy bacon. Warm and hearty, this chowder is perfect for the winter months or a cool summer night. No matter when you choose to make this one-pot meal, be sure to grab a big spoon, because you're going to need it.*

**4 slices bacon, chopped**

**1 onion, diced**

**4 tablespoons minced garlic, divided**

**2 Yukon gold potatoes, chopped**

**16 ounces frozen corn**

**2 cups vegetable broth**

**1 teaspoon dried thyme**

**1 teaspoon sea salt, divided**

**1 teaspoon freshly ground black pepper, divided**

**16 jumbo shrimp, fresh or defrosted from frozen, peeled and deveined**

**1 tablespoon extra-virgin olive oil**

**½ teaspoon red pepper flakes**

**¾ cup heavy (whipping) cream**

**PREP TIME**
10 MINUTES

**TOTAL COOK TIME**
35 MINUTES

**SEAR/SAUTÉ**
5 MINUTES

**APPROX. PRESSURE BUILD**
10 MINUTES

**PRESSURE COOK**
10 MINUTES

**PRESSURE RELEASE**
2 MINUTES

**BROIL**
8 MINUTES

**ACCESSORIES**
REVERSIBLE RACK, PRESSURE LID, CRISPING LID

**GLUTEN-FREE, NUT-FREE, 360 MEAL**

**TIP:** To make this chowder dairy-free, swap out the heavy cream for whole-fat coconut milk. If you want to make this chowder vegetarian, omit the bacon and shrimp and be sure to add 1 tablespoon of oil to the pot in step 2 before adding the onion and garlic.

1.  Select Sear/Sauté and set to Medium High. Select Start/Stop to begin. Allow the pot to preheat for 5 minutes.

2.  Combine the bacon, onion, and 2 tablespoons of garlic in the preheated pot. Cook, stirring occasionally, for 5 minutes. Reserve some of the bacon for garnish.

3.  Add the potatoes, corn, vegetable broth, thyme, ½ teaspoon of salt, and ½ teaspoon of black pepper to the pot. Assemble the Pressure Lid, making sure the pressure release valve is in the Seal position.

4.  Select Pressure and set to High. Set the time to 10 minutes, then select Start/Stop to begin.

5.  While the chowder is cooking, in a medium mixing bowl, toss the shrimp in the remaining 2 tablespoons of garlic, ½ teaspoon of salt, ½ teaspoon of black pepper, the olive oil, and the red pepper flakes.

6. When pressure cooking the chowder is complete, quick release the pressure by moving the pressure release valve to the Vent position. Carefully remove the lid when the pressure has finished releasing.

7. Stir the cream into the chowder. Place the Reversible Rack inside the pot over the chowder, making sure the rack is in the higher position. Place the shrimp on the rack.

8. Close the Crisping Lid. Select Broil and set the time to 8 minutes. Select Start/Stop to begin.

9. When cooking is complete, remove the rack from the pot. Ladle the corn chowder into bowls and top with the shrimp and reserved bacon. Serve immediately.

**Per serving** Calories: 573; Total fat: 34g; Saturated fat: 15g; Cholesterol: 133mg; Sodium: 1172mg; Carbohydrates: 54g; Fiber: 5g; Protein: 18g

# Cajun Stew

SERVES 6

*My husband and I love traveling to New Orleans. While some choose to drink their way through this historic and colorful city, we choose to eat our way through it! Gumbo is the official state cuisine of Louisiana, and while this is a Cajun stew and not a traditional gumbo, it was inspired by the various gumbos we've enjoyed during our trips.*

1 pound sea bass fillets, patted dry and cut into 2-inch chunks

3 tablespoons Cajun seasoning, divided

½ teaspoon sea salt, divided

2 tablespoons extra-virgin olive oil, divided

2 yellow onions, diced

2 bell peppers, diced

4 celery stalks, diced

1 (28-ounce) can diced tomatoes, drained

¼ cup tomato paste

1½ cups vegetable broth

2 pounds large shrimp, peeled and deveined

**PREP TIME**
10 MINUTES

**TOTAL COOK TIME**
28 MINUTES

**SEAR/SAUTÉ**
13 MINUTES

**APPROX. PRESSURE BUILD**
8 MINUTES

**PRESSURE COOK**
5 MINUTES

**PRESSURE RELEASE**
2 MINUTES

**ACCESSORIES**
PRESSURE LID

**DAIRY-FREE, GLUTEN-FREE, NUT-FREE, UNDER 30 MINUTES**

**TIP:** Add a crunchy element to this dish. Place the Reversible Rack into the pot over the stew, making sure the rack is in the higher position. Place 4 slices of French bread on the rack and brush them with olive oil. Bake at 325°F for 6 minutes.

1. Select Sear/Sauté and set to Medium High. Select Start/Stop to begin. Allow the pot to preheat for 5 minutes.

2. Season the sea bass on both sides with 1½ tablespoons of Cajun seasoning and ¼ teaspoon of salt.

3. Put 1 tablespoon of oil and the sea bass in the preheated pot. Sauté, stirring occasionally, for 4 minutes. Remove the fish from the pot and set aside.

4. Add the remaining 1 tablespoon of oil and the onions to the pot. Cook, stirring occasionally, for 3 minutes. Add the bell peppers, celery, and remaining 1½ tablespoons of Cajun seasoning to the pot and cook for an additional 2 minutes.

5. Add the sea bass, diced tomatoes, tomato paste, and broth to the pot. Assemble the Pressure Lid, making sure the pressure release valve is in the Seal position.

6. Select Pressure and set to High. Set the time to 5 minutes, then select Start/Stop to begin.

7. When pressure cooking is complete, quick release the pressure by moving the pressure release valve to the Vent position. Carefully remove the lid when the pressure has finished releasing.

8. Select Sear/Sauté and set to Medium High. Select Start/Stop to begin. Add the shrimp to the pot.

9. Assemble the Pressure Lid, making sure the pressure release valve is in the Vent position. Cover and cook for 4 minutes, or until the shrimp is opaque and cooked through. Season with the remaining ¼ teaspoon of salt and serve.

**Per serving** Calories: 326; Total fat: 9g; Saturated fat: 2g; Cholesterol: 260mg; Sodium: 732mg; Carbohydrates: 13g; Fiber: 3g; Protein: 46g

# Fisherman's Paella

*Paella is a classic Spanish dish with fluffy yellow rice. You can customize it for any kind of palate, topping it with everything from peppers and veggies to chorizo, and of course lobster and shrimp. This version of a seafood paella comes from coastal Spain and calls for a plethora of fresh seafood. And when you make it in the Ninja® Foodi,™ there is no need for a special paella pan or waiting for hours while you cook it on the stove.*

1 tablespoon extra-virgin olive oil

1 pound chorizo, cut into ½-inch slices

1 yellow onion, chopped

4 garlic cloves, minced

½ cup dry white wine

2 cups long-grain white rice

4 cups chicken broth

1½ teaspoons smoked paprika

1 teaspoon turmeric

½ teaspoon sea salt

½ teaspoon freshly ground black pepper

1 pound fresh shrimp, peeled and deveined

1 pound small clams, scrubbed

1 red bell pepper, diced

**PREP TIME**
10 MINUTES

**TOTAL COOK TIME**
30 MINUTES

**SEAR/SAUTÉ**
16 MINUTES

**APPROX. PRESSURE BUILD**
7 MINUTES

**PRESSURE COOK**
5 MINUTES

**PRESSURE RELEASE**
2 MINUTES

**ACCESSORIES**
PRESSURE LID

**DAIRY-FREE, GLUTEN-FREE, NUT-FREE, UNDER 30 MINUTES**

**TIP:** Want to pack this paella with even more seafood? Instead of using a full pound of shrimp, use ½ pound of shrimp and ½ pound of crawfish tails.

1. Select Sear/Sauté and set to Medium High. Select Start/Stop to begin. Allow the pot to preheat for 5 minutes.

2. Put the oil and chorizo in the preheated pot and cook, stirring occasionally, until the meat is brown on both sides, about 3 minutes. Remove the chorizo from the pot and set aside.

3. Add the onion and garlic to the pot. Cook, stirring occasionally, for 5 minutes. Add the wine and stir with a wooden spoon, scraping up any brown bits from the bottom of the pot, and cook for about 2 minutes, until the wine is reduced by half.

4. Add the rice and broth to the pot. Season with the paprika, turmeric, salt, and pepper. Assemble the Pressure Lid, making sure the pressure release valve is in the Seal position.

5. Select Pressure and set to High. Set the time to 5 minutes, then select Start/Stop to begin.

6. When pressure cooking is complete, quick release the pressure by moving the pressure release valve to the Vent position. Carefully remove the lid when the pressure has finished releasing.

7. Select Sear/Sauté and set to Medium High. Select Start/Stop to begin. Add the shrimp and clams to the pot.

8. Assemble the Pressure Lid, making sure the pressure release valve is in the Vent position. Cover and cook for 6 minutes, until the shrimp are pink and opaque and the clams have opened. Discard any unopened clams.

9. Return the chorizo to the pot and add the bell pepper. Stir to combine and serve immediately.

**Per serving** Calories: 1066; Total fat: 50g; Saturated fat: 17g; Cholesterol: 278mg; Sodium: 2425mg; Carbohydrates: 87g; Fiber: 3g; Protein: 60g

# Crispy Fish Tacos

**SERVES 4**

*If there is one thing they know how to do in California, it's fish tacos. A great fish taco is all about the contrast between the crispy fish, the warm tortilla, and the fresh toppings. These tacos are inspired by a little place I found between L.A. and San Diego. Enjoy warm with an ice-cold beer!*

**2 eggs**

**8 ounces Mexican beer**

**1½ cups cornstarch**

**1½ cups all-purpose flour**

**½ tablespoon chili powder**

**1 tablespoon ground cumin**

**½ teaspoon sea salt**

**½ teaspoon freshly ground black pepper**

**1 pound cod, cut into 1½-inch pieces**

**Nonstick cooking spray**

**8 (6-inch round) soft corn tortillas**

PREP TIME
20 MINUTES

TOTAL COOK TIME
15 MINUTES

AIR CRISP
15 MINUTES

ACCESSORIES
COOK & CRISP™ BASKET, CRISPING LID

DAIRY-FREE, NUT-FREE, UNDER 30 MINUTES

1. Place the Cook & Crisp Basket in the pot and close the Crisping Lid. Preheat the unit by selecting Air Crisp, setting the temperature to 375°F and setting the time to 5 minutes.

2. Meanwhile, in a large, shallow bowl, whisk together the eggs and beer. In a separate large bowl, whisk together the cornstarch, flour, chili powder, cumin, salt, and pepper.

3. Coat one piece of cod in the egg mixture, then dredge in the flour mixture, coating on all sides. Place the cod back in the egg mixture to coat, then dredge for a second time in the flour mixture. Repeat with the remaining cod pieces.

4. Spray the preheated Cook & Crisp Basket with nonstick cooking spray. Place the fish in the basket and coat it with cooking spray.

5. Close the Crisping Lid. Select Air Crisp, set the temperature to 375°F, and set the time to 15 minutes. Press Start/Stop to begin.

6. After 8 minutes, open the lid and flip the fish using silicone tongs. Coat with cooking spray and close the lid to resume cooking.

7. After 7 minutes, check the fish for your desired crispiness. Remove the fish from the basket. Arrange on the tortillas and serve with your preferred toppings, such as diced mangos, bell peppers, jalapeños, red onion, crumbled queso fresco, and/or lime juice.

**Per serving** Calories: 623; Total fat: 5g; Saturated fat: 1g; Cholesterol: 154mg; Sodium: 994mg; Carbohydrates: 105g; Fiber: 4g; Protein: 31g

# Fish and Chips

**SERVES 4**

*Typically deep-fried fish and French fries, fish and chips is a seafood favorite in many parts of the world, whether in the middle of London, along the coast of Maine, or on the beaches of New Zealand, each with its own twist, from swapping the fries for potato chips to switching up the type of fish. Here, this classic gets a Ninja® Foodi™ makeover: The fish is Air Crisped instead of fried, so you get all the crispy deliciousness with less oil.*

2 eggs

8 ounces ale beer

1 cup cornstarch

1 cup all-purpose flour

½ tablespoon chili powder

1 tablespoon ground cumin

1 teaspoon sea salt, plus more for seasoning

1 teaspoon freshly ground black pepper, plus more for seasoning

4 (5- to 6-ounce) cod fillets

Nonstick cooking spray

2 russet potatoes, cut into ¼- to ½-inch matchsticks

2 tablespoons vegetable oil

**PREP TIME**
20 MINUTES

**TOTAL COOK TIME**
39 MINUTES

**AIR CRISP**
39 MINUTES

**ACCESSORIES**
COOK & CRISP™ BASKET, CRISPING LID

**DAIRY-FREE, NUT-FREE**

**TIP:** I love using this technique to replicate a deep-fried beer batter. This is as great a technique to use for chicken fingers and nuggets as it is for fish.

1. Place the Cook & Crisp Basket in the pot and close the Crisping Lid. Preheat the unit by selecting Air Crisp, setting the temperature to 375°F, and setting the time to 5 minutes.

2. Meanwhile, in a shallow mixing bowl, whisk together the eggs and beer. In a separate medium bowl whisk together the cornstarch, flour, chili powder, cumin, salt, and pepper.

3. Coat each cod fillet in the egg mixture, then dredge in the flour mixture, coating on all sides.

4. Spray the preheated Cook & Crisp Basket with nonstick cooking spray. Place the fish fillets in the basket and coat them with cooking spray.

5. Close the Crisping Lid. Select Air Crisp, set the temperature to 375°F, and set the time to 15 minutes. Press Start/Stop to begin.

6. Meanwhile, toss the potatoes with the oil and season with salt and pepper.

7. After 15 minutes, check the fish for your desired crispiness. Remove the fish from the basket.

8. Place the potatoes in the Cook & Crisp™ Basket. Close the Crisping Lid. Select Air Crisp, set the temperature to 400ºF, and set the time to 24 minutes. Press Start/Stop to begin.

9. After 12 minutes, open the lid, then lift the basket and shake the fries. Lower the basket back into the pot and close the lid to resume cooking until they reach your desired crispiness.

**Per serving** Calories: 674; Total fat: 11g; Saturated fat: 2g; Cholesterol: 166mg; Sodium: 1299mg; Carbohydrates: 100g; Fiber: 3g; Protein: 35g

# Seafood Pasta all'Arrabbiata

SERVES 4

*Arrabbiata sauce is a punchy sauce made of hot red chiles, tomatoes, and garlicky good-ness. It's simple, but that is the beautiful thing about Italian cuisine—you find quality and elegance in even the simplest recipes. While arrabbiata sauce is delicious on its own, here it coats a variety of seafood and pasta. Pair this recipe with a glass of Pinot Grigio, and your dinner table will be transported to the Mediterranean coast.*

1 tablespoon extra-virgin olive oil

1 onion, diced

4 garlic cloves, minced

16 ounces linguine

1 (24-ounce) jar Arrabbiata sauce

3 cups chicken broth, divided

½ teaspoon sea salt

½ teaspoon freshly ground black pepper

8 ounces shrimp, peeled and deveined

8 ounces scallops

12 mussels, cleaned and debearded

**PREP TIME**
10 MINUTES

**TOTAL COOK TIME**
23 MINUTES

**SEAR/SAUTÉ**
11 MINUTES

**APPROX. PRESSURE BUILD**
8 MINUTES

**PRESSURE COOK**
2 MINUTES

**PRESSURE RELEASE**
2 MINUTES

**ACCESSORIES**
PRESSURE LID

**DAIRY-FREE, NUT-FREE, UNDER 30 MINUTES**

**TIP:** If you don't enjoy spicy dishes but still want to enjoy this seafood pasta dish, dial down the spice by substituting marinara sauce for half or all of the Arrabbiata sauce.

1. Select Sear/Sauté and set to Medium High. Select Start/Stop to begin. Allow the pot to preheat for 5 minutes.

2. Put the oil and onion in the preheated pot and cook for 5 minutes, stirring occasionally. Add the garlic and cook until fragrant, about 1 minute.

3. Break the linguine in half and add to the pot along with the Arrabbiata sauce and 2 cups of broth. Season with the salt and pepper and stir to combine.

4. Assemble the Pressure Lid, making sure the pressure release valve is in the Seal position. Select Pressure and set to High. Set the time to 2 minutes, then select Start/Stop to begin.

5. When pressure cooking is complete, quick release the pressure by moving the pressure release valve to the Vent position. Carefully remove the lid when the pressure has finished releasing.

6. Select Sear/Sauté and set to Medium High. Select Start/Stop to begin. Add the remaining 1 cup of broth, the shrimp, scallops, and mussels to the pot. Stir until all of the seafood is evenly covered by the sauce.

7. Assemble the Pressure Lid, making sure the pressure release valve is in the Vent position. Cover and cook for 5 minutes, until the mussels have opened and the shrimp and scallops are opaque and cooked through. Discard any unopened mussels. Serve.

**Per serving** Calories: 845; Total fat: 16g; Saturated fat: 4g; Cholesterol: 136mg; Sodium: 1539mg; Carbohydrates: 120g; Fiber: 8g; Protein: 50g

# 7
# Poultry Mains

Left: Crispy Chicken Thighs with Roasted Carrots, page 98

# Smoked Paprika
# Whole Roasted Chicken

**SERVES 4**

*Roasting a whole chicken is a skill that every home cook should master, but it can be intimidating. Whether it's a 5-pound chicken or a Thanksgiving turkey, the thought of messing up is enough to keep one from even trying. Luckily, with this recipe, and the Ninja® Foodi™ of course, you are destined for the perfect roast chicken every time: Moist and tender meat on the inside, with golden-brown, crispy skin on the outside.*

1 (4½- to 5-pound) whole chicken

½ cup white wine

Juice of 1 lemon

3 tablespoons extra virgin olive oil

Juice of 2 limes

¼ cup low-sodium soy sauce

2 tablespoons smoked paprika

1½ tablespoons ground cumin

6 cloves garlic, grated

1 tablespoon kosher salt

**PREP TIME**
10 MINUTES

**TOTAL COOK TIME**
42 MINUTES

**APPROX. PRESSURE BUILD**
6 MINUTES

**PRESSURE COOK**
20 MINUTES

**PRESSURE RELEASE**
1 MINUTE

**AIR CRISP**
15 MINUTES

**ACCESSORIES**
COOK & CRISP™ BASKET, PRESSURE LID, CRISPING LID

**NUT-FREE**

**TIP:** If you prefer a simple whole roasted chicken with less spices, see the recipe for The Perfect Roast Chicken (page 17).

1. Discard the neck from inside the chicken cavity and remove any excess fat and leftover feathers. Rinse the chicken inside and out and tie the legs together with cooking twine.

2. Add the wine and lemon juice to the cooking pot. Place the chicken into the Cook & Crisp™ Basket and place the basket in the pot.

3. Assemble the Pressure Lid, making sure the pressure release valve is in the Seal position. Select Pressure and set to High. Set the time to 20 minutes, then select Start/ Stop to begin.

4. When pressure cooking is complete, quick release the pressure by moving the pressure release valve to the Vent position. When the pressure has finished releasing, carefully remove the Pressure Lid.

5. In a small bowl, combine the olive oil, lime juice, soy sauce, paprika, cumin, oregano, garlic and salt and mix until thoroughly combined. Brush the mixture over the chicken.

6. Close the Crisping Lid. Select Air Crisp, set the temperature to 400°F, and set the time to 15 minutes. Select Start/Stop to begin. If you prefer a crispier chicken, add an additional 5-10 minutes.

7. After about 10 minutes, lift the Crisping Lid and sprinkle the chicken with the fresh rosemary. Close the Crisping Lid and continue cooking.

8. Cooking is complete when the internal temperature of the chicken reaches 165°F on a meat thermometer inserted into the thickest part of the meat (it should not touch the bone). Carefully remove the chicken from the basket using the Ninja Roast Lifters or 2 large serving forks.

9. Let the chicken rest for 10 minutes before carving and serving.

**Per serving** Calories: 418; Total fat: 30g; Saturated fat: 12g; Cholesterol: 139mg; Sodium: 1845mg; Carbohydrates: 2g; Fiber: 0g; Protein: 31g

# Crispy Chicken Thighs with Roasted Carrots

**SERVES 4**

*Chicken thighs are a favorite in our house because they are inexpensive but full of flavor. The key to this recipe is using bone-in, skin-on chicken thighs. Using Pressure keeps the meat moist and tender while infusing tons of flavor. Then, the Crisping Lid makes quick work of roasting the carrots and creating the perfect crisp, crackling chicken skin. Say so long to rubbery chicken skin and hello to caramelized perfection!*

**1 cup white rice**

**1½ cups chicken broth**

**4 bone-in, skin-on chicken thighs**

**2 carrots, peeled and cut into ½-by-2-inch pieces**

**2 tablespoons extra-virgin olive oil**

**2 teaspoons poultry spice**

**1 teaspoon sea salt, divided**

**2 teaspoons chopped fresh rosemary**

**PREP TIME**
10 MINUTES

**TOTAL COOK TIME**
22 MINUTES

**APPROX. PRESSURE BUILD**
8 MINUTES

**PRESSURE COOK**
2 MINUTES

**PRESSURE RELEASE**
2 MINUTES

**BROIL**
10 MINUTES

**ACCESSORIES**
REVERSIBLE RACK, PRESSURE LID, CRISPING LID

**DAIRY-FREE, NUT-FREE, UNDER 30 MINUTES, 360 MEAL**

**TIP:** Try other veggies like parsnips, broccoli, or asparagus in place of the carrots in this recipe.

1. Put the rice and chicken broth in the pot.

2. Place the Reversible Rack in the pot, making sure the rack is in the higher position. Place the chicken thighs skin-side up on the rack and arrange the carrots around the chicken. Assemble the Pressure Lid, making sure the pressure release valve is in the Seal position.

3. Select Pressure and set to High. Set the time to 2 minutes, then select Start/Stop to begin.

4. When pressure cooking is complete, quick release the pressure by moving the pressure release valve to the Vent position. Carefully remove the lid when the pressure has finished releasing.

5. Brush the carrots and chicken with the olive oil. Season the chicken evenly with the poultry spice and ½ teaspoon of salt. Season the carrots with the rosemary and remaining ½ teaspoon of salt.

6. Close the Crisping Lid. Select Broil and set the time to 10 minutes. Select Start/Stop to begin.

7. When cooking is complete, check for your desired crispiness and serve the chicken and carrots over the rice.

**Per serving** Calories: 425; Total fat: 18g; Saturated fat: 4g; Cholesterol: 51mg; Sodium: 761mg; Carbohydrates: 48g; Fiber: 6g; Protein: 18g

# Chicken Fried Rice

*Making fried rice at home is a great way to satisfy a craving for takeout while controlling the ingredients. The downside? Too many steps and a sink full of pots and pans. This recipe gives you a quick and easy weeknight meal with the flavors you're craving but without the pile of dishes afterward.*

1 tablespoon extra-virgin olive oil

1 onion, diced

4 garlic cloves, minced

1 pound boneless, skinless chicken breasts, diced

⅛ teaspoon sea salt

⅛ teaspoon freshly ground black pepper

2 cups chicken broth

¼ cup soy sauce

1 cup jasmine rice

1 (16-ounce) bag frozen mixed vegetables

**PREP TIME**
5 MINUTES

**TOTAL COOK TIME**
29 MINUTES

**SEAR/SAUTÉ**
16 MINUTES

**APPROX. PRESSURE BUILD**
8 MINUTES

**PRESSURE COOK**
3 MINUTES

**PRESSURE RELEASE**
2 MINUTES

**ACCESSORIES**
PRESSURE LID

**DAIRY-FREE, NUT-FREE, UNDER 30 MINUTES**

1. Select Sear/Sauté and set to Medium High. Select Start/Stop to begin. Allow the pot to preheat for 5 minutes.

2. Put the oil and onion in the preheated pot and cook for 5 minutes, stirring occasionally. Add the garlic and cook until fragrant, about 1 minute more.

3. Add the chicken to the pot and season with the salt and pepper. Cook for 5 minutes to brown the chicken.

4. Add the chicken broth, soy sauce, and rice to the pot. Assemble the Pressure Lid, making sure the pressure release valve is in the Seal position. Select Pressure and set to High. Set the time to 3 minutes, then select Start/Stop to begin.

5. When pressure cooking is complete, quick release the pressure by moving the pressure release valve to the Vent position. Carefully remove the lid when the pressure has finished releasing.

6. Select Sear/Sauté and set to Medium High. Select Start/Stop to begin. Add the frozen vegetables to the pot. Cook for 5 minutes, stirring occasionally. Serve.

**Per serving** Calories: 461; Total fat: 7g; Saturated fat: 1g; Cholesterol: 69mg; Sodium: 1305mg; Carbohydrates: 60g; Fiber: 6g; Protein: 38g

# Orange Chicken and Broccoli

**SERVES 2**

*Orange chicken has to be one of my favorite Chinese dishes. It is sticky and sweet—a combination I can totally get behind. I love this version because the chicken and broccoli get slightly crispy before being tossed with the sticky sauce, so the texture is amazing. This recipe is also a great make-ahead meal that you can use to meal prep for the week!*

**1 cup long-grain white rice**

**1 cup plus 2 tablespoons water**

**1 head broccoli, trimmed into florets**

**2 tablespoons extra-virgin olive oil, divided**

**¼ teaspoon sea salt**

**¼ teaspoon freshly ground black pepper**

**Nonstick cooking spray**

**4 boneless, skinless chicken tenders**

**¼ cup barbecue sauce**

**¼ cup sweet orange marmalade**

**½ tablespoon soy sauce**

**1 tablespoon sesame seeds, for garnish**

**2 tablespoons sliced scallions, for garnish**

**PREP TIME**
15 MINUTES

**TOTAL COOK TIME**
27 MINUTES

**APPROX. PRESSURE BUILD**
8 MINUTES

**PRESSURE COOK**
2 MINUTES

**PRESSURE RELEASE**
2 MINUTES

**AIR CRISP**
10 MINUTES

**BROIL**
5 MINUTES

**ACCESSORIES**
REVERSIBLE RACK, PRESSURE LID, CRISPING LID

**DAIRY-FREE, NUT-FREE, UNDER 30 MINUTES, 360 MEAL**

1.  Put the rice and water in the pot and stir to combine. Assemble the Pressure Lid, making sure the pressure release valve is in the Seal position. Select Pressure and set to High. Set the time to 2 minutes, then select Start/Stop to begin.

2.  Meanwhile, in a medium mixing bowl, toss the broccoli with 1 tablespoon of olive oil. Season with the salt and black pepper.

3.  When pressure cooking is complete, quick release the pressure by moving the pressure release valve to the Vent position. Carefully remove the lid when the pressure has finished releasing.

4.  Place the Reversible Rack inside the pot over the rice, making sure the rack is in the higher position. Spray the rack with nonstick cooking spray. Place the chicken tenders on the rack and brush them with the remaining 1 tablespoon of olive oil. Arrange the broccoli around the chicken tenders.

5.  Close the Crisping Lid. Select Air Crisp, set the temperature to 400ºF, and set the time to 10 minutes. Press Start/Stop to begin.

6.  Meanwhile, in a medium mixing bowl, stir together the barbecue sauce, orange marmalade, and soy sauce until well combined.

7.  When Air Crisping is complete, coat the chicken with the orange sauce. Use tongs to flip the chicken and coat the other side. Close the Crisping Lid. Select Broil and set the time to 5 minutes. Select Start/Stop to begin.

8.  After cooking is complete, check for your desired crispiness and remove the rack from the pot. The chicken is cooked when its internal temperature reaches 165ºF on a meat thermometer.

9.  Garnish with the sesame seeds and scallions and serve.

**Per serving** Calories: 849; Total fat: 23g; Saturated fat: 3g; Cholesterol: 32mg; Sodium: 1057mg; Carbohydrates: 136g; Fiber: 12g; Protein: 31g

# Chicken Pho

*Pho (pronounced "fuh") is a Vietnamese broth and noodle soup. A good pho starts with the broth, which is traditionally made on the stove. While I love a good pho, I don't have hours to simmer broth on the stove—especially during the week. Using the Ninja® Foodi,™ the broth comes out perfectly comforting and delicious. I cook the chicken straight in the broth to add flavor and tenderize the meat, then I garnish the pho with my favorite toppings.*

1 tablespoon extra-virgin olive oil

1 onion, diced

1½ teaspoons ground coriander

½ teaspoon ground cinnamon

¼ teaspoon ground cardamom

¼ teaspoon ground cloves

1 pound boneless, skinless chicken breasts

1 (1-inch) piece ginger, peeled and chopped

1 lemongrass stalk, trimmed and cut into 2-inch pieces

¼ cup fish sauce

2 cups chicken broth

¼ teaspoon sea salt

1 (16-ounce) package rice vermicelli, prepared according to package directions

Lime wedges, bean sprouts, sliced jalapeño peppers, and/or fresh basil leaves, for garnish (optional)

**PREP TIME**
10 MINUTES

**TOTAL COOK TIME**
29 MINUTES

**SEAR/SAUTÉ**
9 MINUTES

**APPROX. PRESSURE BUILD**
6 MINUTES

**PRESSURE COOK**
13 MINUTES

**PRESSURE RELEASE**
1 MINUTE

**ACCESSORIES**
PRESSURE LID

**DAIRY-FREE, GLUTEN-FREE, NUT-FREE, UNDER 30 MINUTES**

**TIP:** You can easily replace the chicken breast with whatever cut of chicken you have on hand, even frozen chicken. Simply add more time per the chart on page 162. You can also use pork in place of the chicken if you're in the mood for something different.

1. Select Sear/Sauté and set to Medium High. Select Start/Stop to begin. Allow the pot to preheat for 5 minutes.

2. Put the oil and onion in the preheated pot and cook for 3 minutes, stirring occasionally. Add the coriander, cinnamon, cardamom, and cloves to the pot and toast until fragrant, about 1 minute.

3. Add the chicken and cook to brown for 5 minutes.

4. Add the ginger, lemongrass, fish sauce, chicken broth, and salt to the pot. Assemble the Pressure Lid, making sure the pressure release valve is in the Seal position. Select Pressure and set to High. Set the time to 13 minutes, then select Start/Stop to begin.

5. When pressure cooking is complete, quick release the pressure by moving the pressure release valve to the Vent position. Carefully remove the lid when the pressure has finished releasing.

6. Remove and discard the ginger and lemongrass. Remove the chicken from the pot and use two forks to shred the meat.

7. Divide the rice noodles and shredded chicken among bowls and ladle some of the broth into each bowl. Let the soup sit for about 3 minutes to rehydrate the noodles. Garnish each bowl with toppings such as lime wedges, bean sprouts, jalapeño slices, and basil leaves (if using), and serve.

**Per serving**  Calories: 215; Total fat: 6g; Saturated fat: 1g; Cholesterol: 69mg; Sodium: 1781mg; Carbohydrates: 7g; Fiber: 0g; Protein: 30g

# Chicken and Crispy Dumplings

**SERVES 6**

*Chicken and dumplings is comfort food at its best. Tender chicken breasts, plump dumplings, and lots of vegetables in a silky gravy creates a meal that's warm and filling. This version is a twist on the classic, because after the base of the soup is cooked, the dumplings are crisped lightly, adding a delightful crunch to each bite.*

1 tablespoon extra-virgin olive oil

1 yellow onion, chopped

2 celery stalks, diced

2 carrots, diced

1 pound boneless, skinless chicken breasts, cut in 1-inch pieces

2 cups chicken broth

1 teaspoon fresh thyme

½ teaspoon sea salt

½ cup heavy (whipping) cream

1 package refrigerated biscuits, at room temperature

**PREP TIME**
10 MINUTES

**TOTAL COOK TIME**
30 MINUTES

**SEAR/SAUTÉ**
3 MINUTES

**APPROX. PRESSURE BUILD**
8 MINUTES

**PRESSURE COOK**
2 MINUTES

**PRESSURE RELEASE**
2 MINUTES

**BROIL**
15 MINUTES

**ACCESSORIES**
PRESSURE LID, CRISPING LID

**NUT-FREE, UNDER 30 MINUTES**

1. Select Sear/Sauté and set to Medium High. Select Start/Stop to begin. Allow the pot to preheat for 5 minutes.

2. Put the oil and onion in the preheated pot and sauté until the onion is softened, about 3 minutes.

3. Add the celery, carrots, chicken, and broth to the pot. Season with the thyme and salt. Assemble the Pressure Lid, making sure the pressure release valve is in the Seal position.

4. Select Pressure and set to High. Set the time to 2 minutes, then select Start/Stop to begin.

5. When pressure cooking is complete, quick release the pressure by moving the pressure release valve to the Vent position. Carefully remove the lid when the pressure has finished releasing.

6. Stir the cream into the soup. Arrange the biscuits in a single layer on top of the soup.

7. Close the Crisping Lid. Select Broil and set the time to 15 minutes. Select Start/Stop to begin.

8. When cooking is complete, remove the pot from the Ninja® Foodi™ and place it on a heat-resistant surface. Let rest for 10 minutes before serving.

**Per serving** Calories: 366; Total fat: 18g; Saturated fat: 8g; Cholesterol: 73mg; Sodium: 873mg; Carbohydrates: 27g; Fiber: 2g; Protein: 24g

# Cheesy Chicken Enchilada Casserole  V G

*To this day I am amazed by my mother and am in awe of how she always seems to do it all. As a single mom, she not only raised my brother and me like a pro, but she also always had a home-cooked meal on the table. While she had a number of staples during the week, I always used to request chicken enchiladas. I loved the creamy, cheesy filling inside of a crunchy tortilla and, of course, the golden-brown cheese on top. Here, I've re-created all of my favorite things about traditional chicken enchiladas in a casserole so that you can be the hero of dinner, just like my mom.*

1 tablespoon extra-virgin olive oil

1 yellow onion, diced

2 garlic cloves, minced

1 pound boneless, skinless chicken breasts

2 cups enchilada sauce

¼ teaspoon sea salt

¼ teaspoon freshly ground black pepper

1 (15-ounce) can black beans, drained and rinsed

1 (16-ounce) bag frozen corn

8 (6-inch) corn tortillas, each cut into 8 pieces

2 cups shredded Cheddar cheese, divided

**PREP TIME**
10 MINUTES

**TOTAL COOK TIME**
34 MINUTES

**SEAR/SAUTÉ**
6 MINUTES

**APPROX. PRESSURE BUILD**
6 MINUTES

**PRESSURE COOK**
15 MINUTES

**PRESSURE RELEASE**
2 MINUTES

**BROIL**
5 MINUTES

**ACCESSORIES**
PRESSURE LID, CRISPING LID

**GLUTEN-FREE, NUT-FREE**

**TIP:** There are two types of enchilada sauce, green and red. While red is considered more traditional than green, they both work great in this recipe.

1. Select Sear/Sauté and set to Medium High. Select Start/Stop to begin. Allow the pot to preheat for 5 minutes.

2. Put the oil and onion in the preheated pot and cook for 5 minutes, stirring occasionally. Add the garlic and cook until fragrant, about 1 minute more.

3. Add the chicken and enchilada sauce to the pot, and season with the salt and black pepper. Stir to combine.

4. Assemble the Pressure Lid, making sure the pressure release valve is in the Seal position. Select Pressure and set to High. Set the time to 15 minutes, then select Start/Stop to begin.

5. When pressure cooking is complete, quick release the pressure by moving the pressure release valve to the Vent position. Carefully remove the lid when the pressure has finished releasing.

6.  Shred the chicken with silicone tongs. Add the black beans, corn, tortilla pieces, and 1 cup of Cheddar cheese to the pot. Stir to combine.

7.  Arrange the remaining 1 cup of cheese evenly on top of the casserole. Close the Crisping Lid. Select Broil and set the time to 5 minutes. Press Start/Stop to begin.

8.  When cooking is complete, let the casserole sit for 5 minutes before serving.

**Per serving** Calories: 511; Total fat: 17g; Saturated fat: 9g; Cholesterol: 83mg; Sodium: 1081mg; Carbohydrates: 54g; Fiber: 10g; Protein: 38g

Dont use slap you mamma seasoning - a little warm

# Arroz con Pollo

*Early in the development of the Ninja® Foodi,™ we brought in a number of expert chefs to evaluate the product and give us feedback on how to improve it. Throughout the process, what I found most interesting was that even the most experienced chefs kept it simple by pulling together a one-pot meal. Many made a version of chicken and rice—so when I started this book I knew I had to include my own version of this dinnertime staple.*

**2 tablespoons extra-virgin olive oil, divided**

**1 onion, diced**

**1 red bell pepper, diced**

**1 tablespoon chili powder**

**1 teaspoon ground cumin**

**1 teaspoon dried oregano**

**½ teaspoon sea salt**

**1 cup long-grain brown rice**

**¾ cup chicken broth**

**½ cup tomato sauce**

**1 pound bone-in, skin-on chicken thighs**

**Chopped fresh cilantro, for garnish**

**Lime wedges, for serving**

**PREP TIME**
15 MINUTES

**TOTAL COOK TIME**
50 MINUTES

**SEAR/SAUTÉ**
5 MINUTES

**APPROX. PRESSURE BUILD**
8 MINUTES

**PRESSURE COOK**
30 MINUTES

**PRESSURE RELEASE**
2 MINUTES

**BROIL**
5 MINUTES

**ACCESSORIES**
REVERSIBLE RACK, PRESSURE LID, CRISPING LID

**DAIRY-FREE, GLUTEN-FREE, NUT-FREE, 360 MEAL**

**TIP:** Add another serving of vegetables to this recipe by stirring in 8 ounces of frozen peas between steps 5 and 6.

1. Select Sear/Sauté and set to Medium High. Select Start/Stop to begin. Allow the pot to preheat for 5 minutes.

2. Put 1 tablespoon of oil and the onion in the preheated pot and cook for 3 minutes, stirring occasionally. Add the bell pepper, chili powder, cumin, oregano, and salt and cook for 2 minutes more.

3. Add the rice, broth, and tomato sauce to the pot. Place the Reversible Rack inside the pot over the rice, making sure the rack is in the higher position. Place the chicken on the rack.

4. Assemble the Pressure Lid, making sure the pressure release valve is in the Seal position. Select Pressure and set to High. Set the time to 30 minutes, then select Start/Stop to begin.

5. When pressure cooking is complete, quick release the pressure by moving the pressure release valve to the Vent position. Carefully remove the lid when the pressure has finished releasing.

6. Brush the chicken thighs with the remaining 1 tablespoon of oil. Close the Crisping Lid. Select Broil and set the time to 5 minutes. Press Start/Stop to begin.

7. After cooking is complete, check for your desired crispiness and remove the rack from the pot. The chicken is cooked when it reaches an internal temperature of 165°F on a meat thermometer inserted into the thickest part of the meat (it should not touch the bone). Garnish with cilantro and serve with lime wedges.

**Per serving** Calories: 487; Total fat: 24g; Saturated fat: 6g; Cholesterol: 80mg; Sodium: 464mg; Carbohydrates: 46g; Fiber: 4g; Protein: 22g

# Turkey Potpie

*Potpies are a great way to use leftover ingredients to create an intensely satisfying and comforting meal. When I was in college, my mom would always send me back to school after each holiday with a potpie or two. I would pop them in the freezer and take them out when I was craving a home-cooked meal. I hope this recipe brings as much comfort to you as it does to me.*

**4 tablespoons (½ stick) unsalted butter**

**1 onion, diced**

**2 garlic cloves, minced**

**2 pounds boneless turkey breasts, cut into 1-inch cubes**

**2 Yukon gold potatoes, diced**

**1 cup chicken broth**

**½ teaspoon sea salt**

**½ teaspoon freshly ground black pepper**

**1 (16-ounce) bag mixed frozen vegetables**

**½ cup heavy (whipping) cream**

**1 store-bought refrigerated piecrust, at room temperature**

**PREP TIME**
10 MINUTES

**TOTAL COOK TIME**
33 MINUTES

**SEAR/SAUTÉ**
6 MINUTES

**APPROX. PRESSURE BUILD**
6 MINUTES

**PRESSURE COOK**
10 MINUTES

**PRESSURE RELEASE**
1 MINUTE

**BROIL**
10 MINUTES

**ACCESSORIES**
PRESSURE LID, CRISPING LID

**NUT-FREE**

1. Select Sear/Sauté and set to Medium High. Select Start/Stop to begin. Allow the pot to preheat for 5 minutes.

2. Put the butter, onion, and garlic in the preheated pot and sauté until the onion is softened, about 3 minutes.

3. Add the turkey, potatoes, and broth to the pot. Season with the salt and black pepper. Assemble the Pressure Lid, making sure the pressure release valve is in the Seal position.

4. Select Pressure and set to High. Set the time to 10 minutes, then select Start/Stop to begin.

5. When pressure cooking is complete, quick release the pressure by moving the pressure release valve to the Vent position. Carefully remove the lid when the pressure has finished releasing.

6. Select Sear/Sauté and set to Medium High. Select Start/Stop to begin. Add the frozen vegetables and cream to the pot. Stir until the sauce thickens and bubbles, about 3 minutes.

7. Lay the piecrust evenly on top of the filling mixture, folding over the edges if necessary. Make a small cut in the center of the crust so that steam can escape during baking.

8. Close the Crisping Lid. Select Broil and set the time to 10 minutes. Select Start/Stop to begin.

9. When cooking is complete, remove the pot from the Ninja® Foodi™ and it place on a heat-resistant surface. Let the potpie rest for 10 to 15 minutes before serving.

**Per serving** Calories: 667; Total fat: 36g; Saturated fat: 16g; Cholesterol: 147mg; Sodium: 543mg; Carbohydrates: 46g; Fiber: 5g; Protein: 40g

# Turkey Chili and Biscuits

**SERVES 6**

*Building a flavorful chili can take hours on the stove, but with pressure you can cook a hearty chili in just minutes. What I love about this recipe is that you are not only making a stew, but you are also using the Crisping Lid to bake biscuits right on top of the chili, making this a true one-pot meal.*

1 tablespoon extra-virgin olive oil

1 onion, chopped

2 garlic cloves, minced

1½ pounds ground turkey

1 tablespoon ground cumin

1 tablespoon dried oregano

3 (15-ounce) cans cannellini beans, drained and rinsed

4 cups chicken broth

⅛ teaspoon sea salt

⅛ teaspoon freshly ground black pepper

1 package refrigerated biscuits, at room temperature

1. Select Sear/Sauté and set to Medium High. Select Start/Stop to begin. Allow the pot to preheat for 5 minutes.

2. Put the oil, onion, and garlic in the preheated pot and sauté until the onion is softened, about 3 minutes.

3. Add the turkey, cumin, oregano, beans, broth, salt, and black pepper to the pot. Assemble the Pressure Lid, making sure the pressure release valve is in the Seal position.

4. Select Pressure and set to High. Set the time to 10 minutes, then select Start/Stop to begin.

5. When pressure cooking is complete, quick release the pressure by moving the pressure release valve to the Vent position. Carefully remove the lid when the pressure has finished releasing.

**PREP TIME**
10 MINUTES

**TOTAL COOK TIME**
38 MINUTES

**SEAR/SAUTÉ**
3 MINUTES

**APPROX. PRESSURE BUILD**
8 MINUTES

**PRESSURE COOK**
10 MINUTES

**PRESSURE RELEASE**
2 MINUTES

**BROIL**
15 MINUTES

**ACCESSORIES**
PRESSURE LID, CRISPING LID

**DAIRY-FREE, NUT-FREE**

**TIP:** Adding a layer of biscuits is an easy way to add crispy texture to any chili or stew. Try this technique with your favorite slow cooker stews as well as pressure cooker recipes.

6. Arrange the biscuits in a single layer on top of the chili.

7. Close the Crisping Lid. Select Broil and set the time to 15 minutes. Select Start/Stop to begin.

8. When cooking is complete, remove the pot from the Ninja® Foodi™ and place it on a heat-resistant surface. Let the chili and biscuits rest for 10 to 15 minutes before serving.

**Per serving** Calories: 600; Total fat: 19g; Saturated fat: 6g; Cholesterol: 94mg; Sodium: 1528mg; Carbohydrates: 69g; Fiber: 15g; Protein: 41g

# 8

# Beef, Pork & Lamb Mains

Left: Pork Teryaki with Rice, page 122

# French Dip Sandwich

*There is a little café down the street from our house that always has a line. When we venture out to face the crowd for brunch, I follow my personal brunch rule: Always order breakfast at lunch, and a mimosa. My husband, Julien, on the other hand, always orders the French dip. This recipe is dedicated to him. It's full of flavorful, tender beef that will melt in your mouth. You might choose this sandwich over breakfast, too!*

**2 pounds beef rump roast, cut into large chunks**

**1 teaspoon paprika**

**1 teaspoon dried mustard**

**1 teaspoon garlic powder**

**1 teaspoon onion powder**

**½ teaspoon sea salt**

**¼ teaspoon freshly ground black pepper**

**2 cups beef stock**

**1 tablespoon Worcestershire sauce**

**1 teaspoon balsamic vinegar**

**1 loaf French bread, cut into 4 even pieces, then sliced in half**

**8 slices provolone cheese**

**PREP TIME**
10 MINUTES

**TOTAL COOK TIME**
50 MINUTES

**APPROX. PRESSURE BUILD**
8 MINUTES

**PRESSURE COOK**
35 MINUTES

**PRESSURE RELEASE**
2 MINUTES

**AIR CRISP**
5 MINUTES

**ACCESSORIES**
REVERSIBLE RACK, PRESSURE LID, CRISPING LID

**NUT-FREE**

**TIP:** If you're a big fan of garlic, you can brush garlic butter or garlic olive oil on the French bread prior to layering the cheese on top.

1. Place the meat in the bottom of the pot.

2. In a small mixing bowl, stir together the paprika, dried mustard, garlic powder, onion powder, salt, and pepper. Sprinkle this over the chunks of meat in the pot.

3. Add the beef stock, Worcestershire sauce, and balsamic vinegar. Assemble the Pressure Lid, making sure the pressure release valve is in the Seal position.

4. Select Pressure and set to High. Set the time to 35 minutes, then select Start/Stop to begin.

5. When pressure cooking is complete, quick release the pressure by moving the pressure release valve to the Vent position. Carefully remove the lid when the pressure has finished releasing.

6. Remove the meat from the pot and use two forks to shred it.

7. Carefully strain the juice from the pot. This is best done by lining a fine-mesh sieve with cheesecloth. Discard the solids and reserve the juice for dipping.

8. Place the meat back in the bottom of the pot. Place the Reversible Rack inside the pot over the meat, making sure the rack is in the higher position.

9. Arrange the bread on the rack open-side up, and top each piece of bread with 1 slice of provolone cheese.

10. Close the Crisping Lid. Select Air Crisp, set the temperature to 400°F, and set the time to 5 minutes. Press Start/Stop to begin.

11. Remove the bread from the rack. Carefully remove the rack from the pot and use tongs to layer the meat on half of the cheesy bread slices. Top with the remaining cheesy bread slices and serve.

**Per serving** Calories: 794; Total fat: 41g; Saturated fat: 20g; Cholesterol: 120mg; Sodium: 1761mg; Carbohydrates: 58g; Fiber: 2g; Protein: 47g

# Beef Empanadas

SERVES 2

*I remember the first time I made homemade empanadas and I spent hours making and chilling the dough, building the filling, and then assembling and baking them. It was a process! This version is made with gyoza wrappers, and it's easy and delicious. Don't underestimate puff pastry: It is quite versatile and works just as well for empanada crust as it does for dessert. Cheesy on the inside and crispy on the outside, these empanadas are everything you could want in a meal in each convenient bite.*

1 tablespoon extra-virgin olive oil

½ small white onion, finely chopped

¼ pound 80% lean ground beef

1 garlic clove, minced

6 green olives, pitted and chopped

¼ teaspoon paprika

¼ teaspoon ground cumin

⅛ teaspoon ground cinnamon

2 small tomatoes, chopped

8 square gyoza wrappers

1 egg, beaten

**PREP TIME**
15 MINUTES

**TOTAL COOK TIME**
23 MINUTES

**SEAR/SAUTÉ**
9 MINUTES

**AIR CRISP**
14 MINUTES

**ACCESSORIES**
COOK & CRISP™ BASKET, CRISPING LID

**DAIRY-FREE, NUT-FREE, UNDER 30 MINUTES**

**TIP:** Experiment with different flavors for your empanadas by adding vegetables like mushrooms or potatoes, or additional proteins like chorizo or diced Hardboiled Eggs (page 23).

1. Select Sear/Sauté and set to Medium High. Select Start/Stop to begin. Allow the pot to preheat for 5 minutes.

2. Put the oil, onion, ground beef, and garlic in the preheated pot and cook for 5 minutes, stirring occasionally.

3. Stir in the olives, paprika, cumin, and cinnamon and cook for an additional 3 minutes. Add the tomatoes and cook for 1 minute more.

4. Carefully remove the beef mixture from the pot.

5. Place the Cook & Crisp Basket in the pot. Close the Crisping Lid. Preheat the unit by selecting Air Crisp, setting the temperature to 400°F, and setting the time to 5 minutes.

6. While the Ninja® Foodi™ is preheating, arrange the gyoza wrappers on a flat surface. Place 1 to 2 tablespoons of the beef mixture in the center of each wrapper. Brush the edges of the wrapper with the egg and carefully fold in half to form a triangle, pinching the edges together to seal them.

7. Arrange 4 empanadas in a single layer in the preheated Cook & Crisp™ Basket.

8. Close the Crisping Lid. Select Air Crisp, set the temperature to 400ºF, and set the time to 7 minutes. Select Start/Stop to begin. When cooking is complete, remove the empanadas from the basket and transfer to a plate.

9. Repeat steps 7 and 8 with the remaining empanadas.

**Per serving** Calories: 394; Total fat: 23g; Saturated fat: 6g; Cholesterol: 148mg; Sodium: 507mg; Carbohydrates: 30g; Fiber: 3g; Protein: 18g

# Pork Teriyaki with Rice

*I often buy pork tenderloin without any plan for how to cook it, but recently I wanted to turn it into this takeout-inspired meal. The recipe uses just a few simple ingredients you probably already have in the pantry. Use a store-bought teriyaki sauce or make your own. Either way, in less than 30 minutes, you will have a dinner on the table that the whole family will love.*

**1 cup long-grain white rice**

**1 cup water**

**1 head broccoli, trimmed into florets**

**1 tablespoon extra-virgin olive oil**

**¼ teaspoon sea salt**

**¼ teaspoon freshly ground black pepper**

**1 pork tenderloin, trimmed and cut into 1-inch pieces**

**1 cup teriyaki sauce**

**Nonstick cooking spray**

**Sesame seeds, for garnish**

*[handwritten: or soy sauce, ginger + honey]*

**PREP TIME**
10 MINUTES

**TOTAL COOK TIME**
24 MINUTES

**APPROX. PRESSURE BUILD**
8 MINUTES

**PRESSURE COOK**
2 MINUTES

**PRESSURE RELEASE**
2 MINUTES

**BROIL**
12 MINUTES

**ACCESSORIES**
REVERSIBLE RACK, PRESSURE LID, CRISPING LID

**DAIRY-FREE, NUT-FREE, UNDER 30 MINUTES, 360 MEAL**

**TIP:** Swap out the broccoli for any fresh veggies you have in the crisper. Carrots, Brussels sprouts, or green beans would also work great in this recipe.

1. Put the rice and water in the pot and stir to combine. Assemble the Pressure Lid, making sure the pressure release valve is in the Seal position. Select Pressure and set to High. Set the time to 2 minutes, then select Start/Stop to begin.

2. Meanwhile, in a large mixing bowl, toss the broccoli with the olive oil. Season with the salt and black pepper. In a medium mixing bowl, toss the pork with the teriyaki sauce until well coated.

3. When pressure cooking of the rice is complete, quick release the pressure by moving the pressure release valve to the Vent position. Carefully remove the lid when the pressure has finished releasing.

4. Place the Reversible Rack inside the pot over the rice, making sure the rack is in the higher position. Spray the rack with cooking spray. Place the pork pieces on the rack. Arrange the broccoli around the pork.

5. Close the Crisping Lid. Select Broil and set the time to 12 minutes. Press Start/Stop to begin.

6. After cooking is complete, check for your desired crispiness and remove the rack from the pot. Serve the pork and broccoli over the rice, garnished with sesame seeds.

**Per serving** Calories: 466; Total fat: 9g; Saturated fat: 2g; Cholesterol: 82mg; Sodium: 3023mg; Carbohydrates: 58g; Fiber: 5g; Protein: 38g

# Mongolian Beef and Broccoli

**SERVES 4**

*Too often, dinner appears so daunting that we choose takeout instead—but the truth is that a delicious dinner can be on your table faster than delivery can. This easy "takeout fake-out" recipe takes just 30 minutes to cook. Crispy, sweet, and full of garlic and ginger, it tastes like it was picked up from your favorite Chinese restaurant.*

**1 tablespoon extra-virgin olive oil**

**2 pounds flank steak, cut into ¼-inch-thick strips**

**4 garlic cloves, minced**

**½ cup soy sauce**

**½ cup water, plus 3 tablespoons**

**⅔ cup dark brown sugar**

**½ teaspoon minced fresh ginger**

**2 tablespoons cornstarch**

**1 head broccoli, trimmed into florets**

**3 scallions, thinly sliced**

**PREP TIME**
10 MINUTES

**TOTAL COOK TIME**
30 MINUTES

**SEAR/SAUTÉ**
12 MINUTES

**APPROX. PRESSURE BUILD**
6 MINUTES

**PRESSURE COOK**
10 MINUTES

**PRESSURE RELEASE**
2 MINUTES

**ACCESSORIES**
PRESSURE LID

**DAIRY-FREE, NUT-FREE, UNDER 30 MINUTES**

**TIP:** Make a batch of white rice following the chart on page 159 to serve alongside the beef and broccoli.

1.  Select Sear/Sauté and set to Medium High. Select Start/Stop to begin. Allow the pot to preheat for 5 minutes.

2.  Put the oil and beef in the preheated pot and sear the beef strips on both sides, about 5 minutes total. Remove from the pot and set aside.

3.  Add the garlic to the pot and sauté for 1 minute.

4.  Add the soy sauce, ½ cup of water, the brown sugar, and ginger to the pot. Stir to combine. Return the beef to the pot.

5.  Assemble the Pressure Lid, making sure the pressure release valve is in the Seal position. Select Pressure and set to High. Set the time to 10 minutes, then select Start/Stop to begin.

6.  Meanwhile, in a small mixing bowl whisk together the cornstarch and remaining 3 tablespoons of water.

7.  When pressure cooking is complete, quick release the pressure by moving the pressure release valve to the Vent position. Carefully remove the lid when the pressure has finished releasing.

8. Select Sear/Sauté and set to Medium Low. Select Start/ Stop to begin. Add the cornstarch mixture to the pot, stirring continuously until the sauce comes to a simmer.

9. Add the broccoli to the pot, stirring to coat it evenly in the sauce, and cook for another 5 minutes.

10. Once cooking is complete, garnish with the scallions.

**Per serving** Calories: 628; Total fat: 18g; Saturated fat: 6g; Cholesterol: 94mg; Sodium: 2182mg; Carbohydrates: 55g; Fiber: 4g; Protein: 62g

# Pita Bread Pizza with Sausage and Peppers

SERVES 4

*I go to a gym located right above a grocery store, and I often stop in after working out to pick up a few groceries and something quick for dinner. The market sells a mini pizza with a crust made from pita bread. I decided I would try to make my own version. The assembly is so simple you can personalize one for every person in the family. This version is topped with sausage and peppers, but you could use pepperoni and cheese, or ham and pineapple instead.*

**4 whole-wheat pitas**

**Nonstick cooking spray**

**½ cup canned crushed tomatoes, divided**

**1 green bell pepper, sliced, divided**

**½ pound sweet Italian sausage, casings removed, meat cooked and crumbled, divided**

**1 cup shredded mozzarella cheese, divided**

**1 teaspoon red pepper flakes, divided**

**1 tablespoon chopped fresh parsley, for garnish**

**PREP TIME**
15 MINUTES

**TOTAL COOK TIME**
28 MINUTES

**AIR CRISP**
16 MINUTES

**BROIL**
12 MINUTES

**ACCESSORIES**
REVERSIBLE RACK,
CRISPING LID

**NUT-FREE,
UNDER 30 MINUTES**

**TIP:** If you prefer a crispier crust, toast both sides of the pita prior to adding the toppings. If you prefer a less crispy crust, skip steps 2 and 3.

1. Place the Reversible Rack in the pot. Close the Crisping Lid. Preheat the unit by selecting Air Crisp, setting the temperature to 400ºF, and setting the time to 5 minutes.

2. Spray one side of a pita with cooking spray and place on the preheated rack, cooking spray–side up.

3. Close the Crisping Lid. Select Air Crisp, set the temperature to 400ºF, and set the time to 4 minutes. Select Start/Stop to begin.

4. Remove the pita from the rack and turn it over so it's crispy-side down. Top the pita with 2 tablespoons of crushed tomatoes, a quarter of the bell pepper, 2 ounces of sausage, ¼ cup of mozzarella cheese, and ¼ tablespoon of red pepper flakes.

5. Close the Crisping Lid. Select Broil and set the time to 3 minutes. Select Start/Stop to begin.

6. After cooking is complete, check for your desired crispiness, adding more time if needed, and remove the pita pizza from the rack.

7. Repeat steps 2 through 6 with the remaining pitas, crushed tomatoes, bell pepper, sausage, cheese, and red pepper flakes. Top each pizza with some of the parsley and serve.

**Per serving** Calories: 441; Total fat: 23g; Saturated fat: 9g; Cholesterol: 63mg; Sodium: 914mg; Carbohydrates: 39g; Fiber: 6g; Protein: 22g

# Barbecue Pork Chops

**SERVES 4**

*Pork chops are a tricky cut of meat; they can go from tender to overcooked in the blink of an eye. But what if I told you that you could have perfectly cooked, perfectly tender pork chops every time? Say so long to dinners of overcooked shoe leather, and say hello to these tender yet crisp barbecue pork chops. This recipe is sure to get pork chops back into your weeknight meal rotation!*

3 tablespoons brown sugar

1 tablespoon sea salt

1 tablespoon freshly ground black pepper

1½ tablespoons smoked paprika

2 teaspoons garlic powder

4 (6-ounce) bone-in pork chops

1 tablespoon extra-virgin olive oil

1½ cups chicken broth

4 tablespoons barbecue sauce, divided

**PREP TIME**
5 MINUTES

**TOTAL COOK TIME**
48 MINUTES

**SEAR/SAUTÉ**
20 MINUTES

**APPROX. PRESSURE BUILD**
8 MINUTES

**PRESSURE COOK**
5 MINUTES

**PRESSURE RELEASE**
12 MINUTES

**BROIL**
3 MINUTES

**ACCESSORIES**
COOK & CRISP™ BASKET, PRESSURE LID, CRISPING LID

**DAIRY-FREE, GLUTEN-FREE, NUT-FREE**

**TIP:** Turn this into a full meal: Remove the pork chops from the basket and drain the pot. Then add broccoli florets or Brussels sprouts that have been tossed in olive oil and seasoned with salt and pepper. While the pork chops rest, cook the veggies on Air Crisp at 390°F for 12 to 18 minutes.

1. Select Sear/Sauté and set to High. Select Start/Stop to begin. Allow the pot to preheat for 5 minutes.

2. Meanwhile, in a small mixing bowl combine the brown sugar, salt, black pepper, paprika, and garlic powder. Season both sides of the pork chops with this seasoning mix.

3. Put the oil in the preheated pot and sear the pork chops, one at a time, on both sides, about 5 minutes per chop, then set aside.

4. Add the chicken broth to the pot and, using a wooden spoon, scrape up the brown bits from the bottom of the pot. Place the Cook & Crisp Basket in the pot. Place the pork chops in the basket and brush them with 2 tablespoons of barbecue sauce.

5. Assemble the Pressure Lid, making sure the pressure release valve is in the Seal position. Select Pressure and set to High. Set the time to 5 minutes, then select Start/Stop to begin.

6. When pressure cooking is complete, allow the pressure to naturally release for 10 minutes, then quick release any remaining pressure by moving the pressure release valve to the Vent position. Carefully remove the lid when the pressure has finished releasing.

7. Brush the pork chops with the remaining 2 tablespoons of barbecue sauce. Close the Crisping Lid. Select Broil and set the time to 3 minutes. Press Start/Stop to begin.

8. After cooking is complete, check for your desired crispiness and remove the pork from the basket.

**Per serving** Calories: 615; Total fat: 45g; Saturated fat: 15g; Cholesterol: 124mg; Sodium: 2143mg; Carbohydrates: 21g; Fiber: 1g; Protein: 29g

# Baked Ziti with Meat Sauce

**SERVES 4**

*Perhaps my favorite baked pasta dish, even more so than lasagna, is baked ziti with meat sauce. But there are too many pots and pans involved! You need one pot to cook the ziti, another to cook the meat sauce, and a baking dish to pull it all together. I love this Ninja® Foodi™ version because I get all of the flavor and texture of homemade baked ziti but with only one pot to clean.*

1 tablespoon extra-virgin olive oil

2 pounds ground beef

2 (24-ounce) jars marinara sauce

1 cup water

1 cup dry red wine

1 (16-ounce) box ziti

½ teaspoon garlic powder

½ teaspoon sea salt

1 cup ricotta cheese

1 cup shredded mozzarella cheese

½ cup chopped fresh parsley

1. Select Sear/Sauté and set to High. Select Start/Stop to begin. Allow the pot to preheat for 5 minutes.

2. Put the oil in the preheated pot, then add the ground beef and cook for 5 to 8 minutes, or until browned and cooked through.

3. Add the marinara sauce, water, wine, and ziti to the pot, stirring to combine. Season with the garlic powder and salt.

4. Assemble the Pressure Lid, making sure the pressure release valve is in the Seal position. Select Pressure and set to Low. Set the time to 2 minutes, then select Start/Stop to begin.

5. When pressure cooking is complete, allow the pressure to naturally release for 10 minutes, then quick release any remaining pressure by moving the pressure release valve to the Vent position. Carefully remove the lid when the pressure has finished releasing.

**PREP TIME**
15 MINUTES

**TOTAL COOK TIME**
32 MINUTES

**SEAR/SAUTÉ**
8 MINUTES

**APPROX. PRESSURE BUILD**
8 MINUTES

**PRESSURE COOK**
2 MINUTES

**PRESSURE RELEASE**
11 MINUTES

**BROIL**
3 MINUTES

**ACCESSORIES**
PRESSURE LID, CRISPING LID

**NUT-FREE**

**TIP:** I love the flavor that wine adds to this dish, but if you prefer to omit it, you can use beef stock in its place. You can also substitute the marinara sauce with your favorite pasta sauce if you prefer.

6. Stir in the ricotta, then evenly top the pasta with the mozzarella cheese.

7. Close the Crisping Lid. Select Broil, and set the time to 3 minutes. Select Start/Stop to begin. Cook for 3 minutes, or until the cheese is melted, bubbly, and slightly browned.

8. Top with the parsley and serve immediately.

**Per serving** Calories: 1186; Total fat: 44g; Saturated fat: 20g; Cholesterol: 162mg; Sodium: 1466mg; Carbohydrates: 119g; Fiber: 9g; Protein: 66g

# Short Ribs with Roasted Sweet Potatoes

**SERVES 4**

*Short ribs are super "in"—they seem to be on just about every menu. You don't need a reservation to hop on the short rib train, though, because they are super easy to make at home. This relatively inexpensive cut of meat is perfect for a pressure cooker because the meat becomes remarkably tender and flavorful. Serve with a side of roasted veggies, or purée the veggies and serve the short ribs on top just like at the trendiest of restaurants.*

**4 (8-ounce) bone-in beef short ribs, trimmed of excess fat and silverskin**

**1 teaspoon sea salt, divided**

**1 teaspoon freshly ground black pepper, divided**

**2 tablespoons extra-virgin olive oil, divided**

**1 onion, chopped**

**½ cup beef broth**

**2 tablespoons brown sugar**

**3 garlic cloves, minced**

**2 tablespoons minced fresh thyme, divided**

**2 sweet potatoes, peeled and cut into 1-inch pieces**

**PREP TIME**
10 MINUTES

**TOTAL COOK TIME**
1 HOUR 20 MINUTES

**SEAR/SAUTÉ**
15 MINUTES

**APPROX. PRESSURE BUILD**
8 MINUTES

**PRESSURE COOK**
40 MINUTES

**PRESSURE RELEASE**
2 MINUTES

**BAKE/ROAST**
15 MINUTES

**ACCESSORIES**
REVERSIBLE RACK, PRESSURE LID, CRISPING LID

**DAIRY-FREE, GLUTEN-FREE, NUT-FREE**

1. Select Sear/Sauté and set to High. Select Start/Stop to begin. Allow the pot to preheat for 5 minutes.

2. Meanwhile, season the short ribs on all sides with ½ teaspoon of salt and ½ teaspoon of pepper.

3. Put 1 tablespoon of oil and the seasoned short ribs in the preheated pot. Cook until the meat is browned on all sides, about 10 minutes total.

4. Add the onion, broth, brown sugar, garlic, and 1 tablespoon of thyme to the pot. Assemble the Pressure Lid, making sure the pressure release valve is in the Seal position.

5. Select Pressure and set to High. Set the time to 40 minutes, then select Start/Stop to begin.

6. In a large mixing bowl, toss the sweet potatoes with the remaining 1 tablespoon of oil, 1 tablespoon of thyme, ½ teaspoon of salt, and ½ teaspoon of pepper.

7. When pressure cooking is complete, quick release the pressure by moving the pressure release valve to the Vent position. Carefully remove the lid when the pressure has finished releasing.

8. Place the Reversible Rack inside the pot over the ribs, making sure the rack is in the higher position. Place the sweet potatoes on the rack.

9. Close the Crisping Lid. Select Bake/Roast, set the temperature to 350°F, and set the time to 15 minutes. Select Start/Stop to begin.

10. Once the sweet potatoes are tender and roasted, remove them and the short ribs from the pot and set aside.

11. Select Sear/Sauté and set to High. Bring the liquid in the pot to a simmer for 5 minutes. Transfer the sauce to a bowl and let sit for 2 minutes, then spoon off the top layer of fat.

12. Serve the sauce with the sweet potatoes and ribs.

**Per serving** Calories: 548; Total fat: 30g; Saturated fat: 11g; Cholesterol: 132mg; Sodium: 826mg; Carbohydrates: 24g; Fiber: 3g; Protein: 45g

# Steak and Baked Sweet Potatoes

SERVES 4

*When we moved, we upgraded from a tiny galley kitchen to a large kitchen with tons of space. That move came with a downsizing of outdoor space, and we were left with no space for a grill. Now I don't have to miss out on grilling season, because the Ninja® Foodi™ cooks steak to perfection. Be sure to keep an eye on your steak in the pot just as you would on the grill so that it is cooked to your desired doneness each time.*

**4 (8-ounce, 1-inch-thick) ribeye steaks**

**4 sweet potatoes**

**1 tablespoon extra-virgin olive oil**

**1 teaspoon sea salt, divided**

**1 teaspoon freshly ground black pepper, divided**

**Nonstick cooking spray**

**Steak sauce, for serving**

**PREP TIME**
5 MINUTES

**TOTAL COOK TIME**
48 MINUTES

**AIR CRISP**
48 MINUTES

**ACCESSORIES**
COOK & CRISP™ BASKET, CRISPING LID

**DAIRY-FREE, GLUTEN-FREE, NUT-FREE**

1. Let the steaks come to room temperature.

2. Place the Cook & Crisp Basket in the pot. Close the Crisping Lid. Preheat the unit by selecting Air Crisp, setting the temperature to 390°F, and setting the time to 5 minutes.

3. Meanwhile, pierce the sweet potatoes several times with a fork and coat them all over with the olive oil.

4. Place the sweet potatoes in the preheated Cook & Crisp Basket and season them with ½ teaspoon of salt and ½ teaspoon of black pepper.

5. Close the Crisping Lid. Select Air Crisp, set the temperature to 400°F, and set the time to 40 minutes. Select Start/Stop to begin.

6. Season the steak on both sides with the remaining ½ teaspoon of salt and ½ teaspoon of black pepper.

7. When cooking is complete, check that the sweet potatoes are fork tender and use tongs to remove them from the basket.

8. Coat the Cook & Crisp Basket with cooking spray. Place the steaks in the basket.

9. Close the Crisping Lid. Select Air Crisp, set the temperature to 400ºF, and set the time to 8 minutes. Select Start/Stop to begin.

10. When cooking is complete, check the steaks for your desired doneness and add more time if needed. Remove the steaks from the basket and let rest for 5 minutes.

11. Serve the steaks alongside the baked sweet potatoes with your favorite steak sauce.

**Per serving** Calories: 504; Total fat: 22g; Saturated fat: 8g; Cholesterol: 132mg; Sodium: 794mg; Carbohydrates: 26g; Fiber: 4g; Protein: 47g

# Barbecue Baby Back Ribs

## SERVES 4

*Perhaps one of the most exciting things you can make in the Ninja® Foodi™ is restaurant-style barbecue. Coined "Quick-Cue," a combination of Pressure and Air Crisp is used to quickly tenderize the meat and then crisp it to add a barbecue-style bark on the outside. Now you can make restaurant-quality barbecue ribs in under an hour all year long!*

3 tablespoons brown sugar

1 tablespoon sea salt

1 tablespoon freshly ground black pepper

1½ tablespoons smoked paprika

2 teaspoons garlic powder

1 (2- to 3-pound) rack baby back ribs, cut into quarters

1 cup beer, preferably a Kentucky bourbon barrel ale

1 cup barbecue sauce

1. In a small mixing bowl, combine the brown sugar, salt, black pepper, paprika, and garlic powder. Season both sides of the ribs with the seasoning mix.

2. Pour the beer into the pot. Place the ribs into the Cook & Crisp Basket and place the basket in the pot.

3. Assemble the Pressure Lid, making sure the pressure release valve is in the Seal position. Select Pressure and set to High. Set the time to 10 minutes, then select Start/Stop to begin.

4. When pressure cooking is complete, quick release the pressure by turning the pressure release valve to the Vent position. Carefully remove the lid when the pressure has finished releasing.

**PREP TIME**
10 MINUTES

**TOTAL COOK TIME**
35 MINUTES

**APPROX. PRESSURE BUILD**
8 MINUTES

**PRESSURE COOK**
10 MINUTES

**PRESSURE RELEASE**
2 MINUTES

**AIR CRISP**
15 MINUTES

**ACCESSORIES**
COOK & CRISP™ BASKET, PRESSURE LID, CRISPING LID

**DAIRY-FREE, NUT-FREE**

**TIP:** Using St. Louis Ribs? Increase the cook time in step 3 to 18 minutes under pressure.

5. Close the Crisping Lid. Select Air Crisp, set the temperature to 400ºF, and set the time to 15 minutes. Select Start/Stop to begin.

6. After 10 minutes, open the lid and liberally brush the ribs with the barbecue sauce. Close the lid to resume cooking for 5 more minutes.

**Per serving** Calories: 808; Total fat: 54g; Saturated fat: 20g; Cholesterol: 184mg; Sodium: 2619mg; Carbohydrates: 37g; Fiber: 1g; Protein: 37g

# Rosemary-Braised Lamb Shanks

**SERVES 4**

*Cooking lamb can be intimidating, but the truth is, cooking it is a fairly hands-off process that even the most novice of cooks can master. These flavorful, tender lamb shanks are braised to perfection with vegetables in a rich broth. This is definitely a meal for the most special of occasions.*

2 lamb shanks

½ teaspoon sea salt

½ teaspoon freshly ground black pepper

2 tablespoons extra-virgin olive oil, divided

1 onion, chopped

4 garlic cloves, minced

2 carrots, chopped

2 celery stalks, chopped

1 (14-ounce) can diced tomatoes, undrained

3½ cups beef broth

2 rosemary sprigs

**PREP TIME**
10 MINUTES

**TOTAL COOK TIME**
1 HOUR

**SEAR/SAUTÉ**
18 MINUTES

**APPROX. PRESSURE BUILD**
10 MINUTES

**PRESSURE COOK**
30 MINUTES

**PRESSURE RELEASE**
2 MINUTES

**ACCESSORIES**
PRESSURE LID

**DAIRY-FREE, GLUTEN-FREE, NUT-FREE**

**TIP:** If you are serving only two people and prefer a fancier presentation, don't shred the meat; instead, serve the lamb shanks whole over the vegetables and broth.

1. Select Sear/Sauté and set to High. Select Start/Stop to begin. Allow the pot to preheat for 5 minutes.

2. Meanwhile, season the lamb shanks on all sides with the salt and black pepper.

3. Put 1 tablespoon of oil and the seasoned lamb shanks in the preheated pot. Cook until browned on all sides, about 10 minutes total. Remove the lamb shanks and set aside.

4. Add the remaining 1 tablespoon of oil, the onion, and the garlic to the pot. Cook, stirring occasionally, for 5 minutes. Add the carrots and celery and cook for 3 minutes more.

5. Add the tomatoes, broth, and rosemary to the pot. Return the lamb shanks to the pot. Assemble the Pressure Lid, making sure the pressure release valve is in the Seal position.

6. Select Pressure and set to High. Set the time to 30 minutes, then select Start/Stop to begin.

7. When pressure cooking is complete, quick release the pressure by moving the pressure release valve to the Vent position. Carefully remove the lid when the pressure has finished releasing.

8. Discard the rosemary sprigs and remove the lamb shanks. Coarsely shred the lamb.

9. Serve the lamb over the vegetables and broth.

**Per serving** Calories: 736; Total fat: 48g; Saturated fat: 20g; Cholesterol: 198mg; Sodium: 974mg; Carbohydrates: 13g; Fiber: 3g; Protein: 61g

# 9

# Desserts, Breads & Rolls

Left: Strawberry Toaster Pastries, page 150

# Dinner Rolls

*Whenever we host a dinner party or entertain, I love to impress guests with homemade dinner rolls. I find that this little step adds a special touch to the meal. Nothing is quite the same as warm, fresh homemade rolls. Serve these with dinner or cut them in half for the perfect slider roll.*

**4 tablespoons (½ stick) plus 1 tablespoon cold unsalted butter, plus more at room temperature for greasing**

**3½ cups all-purpose flour**

**1 cup whole milk**

**1 tablespoon extra-virgin olive oil**

**1 tablespoon coconut oil**

**½ package (1⅛ teaspoons) active dry yeast**

**Nonstick cooking spray**

**¼ teaspoon sea salt**

**PREP TIME**
15 MINUTES, PLUS 1 HOUR 30 MINUTES FOR THE DOUGH TO RISE

**TOTAL COOK TIME**
20 MINUTES

**SEAR/SAUTÉ**
5 MINUTES

**BAKE/ROAST**
15 MINUTES

**ACCESSORIES**
REVERSIBLE RACK, CRISPING LID

**NUT-FREE, VEGETARIAN**

**TIP:** This simple recipe can easily be customized for any occasion. Top the rolls with chopped herbs, garlic, and butter, or with Parmesan cheese. You can even add cinnamon and sugar to the dough and top with caramel sauce for a simple pull-apart monkey bread.

1. In a large mixing bowl, use a pastry cutter or two forks to cut the butter into the flour, breaking up the cold butter into little pieces, until the mixture resembles coarse cornmeal.

2. Put the milk, olive oil, and coconut oil in the pot. Select Sear/Sauté and set to Medium High. Select Start/Stop to begin. Bring to a gentle simmer, about 5 minutes, then press the Start/Stop button to turn off Sear/Sauté.

3. Pour the milk mixture into the flour mixture and stir in the yeast. Mix together until a dough forms.

4. Transfer the dough to a clean work surface dusted with flour and knead it by hand for about 5 minutes.

5. Wipe out the pot, then lightly grease it with butter. Place the kneaded dough in the pot. Cover the dough with plastic wrap and let it rise in a warm place until doubled in size, about 1 hour. Knead the dough again for about 5 minutes, then let it rise a second time for 30 minutes.

6. Turn the dough out onto a floured work surface and divide it evenly into 6 or 12 pieces. Shape each piece into a small ball and place in the Multi-Purpose Pan or an 8-inch baking pan greased with nonstick cooking spray. The rolls should be touching.

7. Close the Crisping Lid. Preheat the unit by selecting Bake/Roast, setting the temperature to 360ºF, and setting the time to 5 minutes. Select Start/Stop to begin.

8. Place the pan on the Reversible Rack, making sure the rack is in the lower position. Place the rack with the pan in the preheated pot.

9. Sprinkle the rolls with the salt, then close the Crisping Lid. Select Bake/Roast, set the temperature to 360ºF, and set the time to 15 minutes. Select Start/Stop to begin.

10. When cooking is complete, allow the rolls to cool, then pull apart and serve.

**Per serving** Calories: 424; Total fat: 18g; Saturated fat: 10g; Cholesterol: 34mg; Sodium: 1041mg; Carbohydrates: 56g; Fiber: 2g; Protein: 9g

# Garlic Bread

SERVES 8

*Garlic bread is a toasty piece of deliciousness that makes a delightful addition to just about any Italian-inspired dinner. Whether served alongside a bowl of pasta, dipped into leftover sauce, or turned into croutons for a salad, garlic bread is never a bad idea. And while there is no wrong way to make it, in my opinion this is the best way.*

**2 eggs**
**¼ cup milk**
**½ French baguette, cut into 8 pieces**

**2 tablespoons extra-virgin olive oil**
**2 teaspoons garlic purée**
**1 teaspoon dried parsley**

**PREP TIME**
5 MINUTES

**TOTAL COOK TIME**
8 MINUTES

**AIR CRISP**
8 MINUTES

**ACCESSORIES**
REVERSIBLE RACK, CRISPING LID

**NUT-FREE, VEGETARIAN, UNDER 30 MINUTES**

1. Place the Reversible Rack in the pot and close the Crisping Lid. Preheat the pot by selecting Air Crisp, setting the temperature to 375°F, and setting the time to 3 minutes. Press Start/Stop to begin.

2. Meanwhile, in a large mixing bowl, whisk together the eggs and milk. Place the bread in the egg mixture and coat each piece on both sides. In a small mixing bowl, mix together the olive oil, garlic purée, and parsley.

3. Place 4 pieces of bread on the preheated rack. Brush the top of each piece with the garlic mixture.

4. Close the Crisping Lid. Select Air Crisp, set the temperature to 375°F, and set the time to 2 minutes. Press Start/Stop to begin.

5. Open the lid and flip the bread. Brush with more of the garlic mixture. Close the lid and select Air Crisp, set the temperature to 375°F, and set the time to 2 minutes. Press Start/Stop to begin.

6. When cooking is complete, remove the garlic bread from the pot and transfer to a plate.

7. Repeat steps 3 through 6 with the remaining pieces of bread. Serve immediately while the garlic bread is warm.

**Per serving** Calories: 146; Total fat: 5g; Saturated fat: 1g; Cholesterol: 54mg; Sodium: 229mg; Carbohydrates: 19g; Fiber: 1g; Protein: 6g

# Zucchini Bread

**SERVES 6**

*A slice of zucchini bread is perfect for a late-night snack or for breakfast with a mug of hot black coffee. Enjoy the bread warm, straight from the Ninja® Foodi,™ or at room temperature a few days later.*

2 eggs

8 tablespoons (1 stick) unsalted butter, melted

1⅓ cups sugar

1 teaspoon vanilla extract

1 teaspoon ground cinnamon

⅛ teaspoon ground nutmeg

½ teaspoon baking soda

¼ teaspoon baking powder

½ teaspoon sea salt

1½ cups all-purpose flour

1 cup grated zucchini

Nonstick cooking spray

**PREP TIME**
15 MINUTES

**TOTAL COOK TIME**
40 MINUTES

**BAKE/ROAST**
40 MINUTES

**ACCESSORIES**
REVERSIBLE RACK, CRISPING LID

**NUT-FREE, VEGETARIAN**

**TIP:** Take this recipe up a notch by stirring ½ cup of chocolate chips into the batter along with the shredded zucchini in step 3. You can also add walnuts, pecans, or dried cranberries.

1. Close the Crisping Lid. Preheat the unit by selecting Bake/Roast, setting the temperature to 325ºF, and setting the time to 5 minutes. Select Start/Stop to begin.

2. Meanwhile, in a large mixing bowl, combine the eggs, butter, sugar, and vanilla. Add the cinnamon, nutmeg, baking soda, baking powder, and salt and stir to combine. Add the flour, a little at a time, stirring until combined.

3. Wring out the excess water from the zucchini and fold it into the batter.

4. Grease the Loaf Pan or another loaf pan with cooking spray and pour in the batter. Place the pan on the Reversible Rack, making sure the rack is in the lower position. Place the rack in the pot.

5. Close the Crisping Lid. Select Bake/Roast, set the temperature to 325ºF, and set the time to 40 minutes. Select Start/Stop to begin.

6. When cooking is complete, remove the loaf pan from the pot and place it on a cooling rack. Allow the zucchini bread to cool for 30 minutes before slicing and serving.

**Per serving** Calories: 445; Total fat: 17g; Saturated fat: 10g; Cholesterol: 111mg; Sodium: 734mg; Carbohydrates: 68g; Fiber: 1g; Protein: 5g

# Cinnamon-Sugar Bites

**SERVES 4**

*These scrumptious little bites bring me right back to my childhood. When I was growing up, my family went to church every Sunday, and after mass, everyone congregated in the big hall. The adults would sip coffee and catch up with one another, while the kids devoured doughnut holes. I give these bites a little upgrade with a cinnamon-sugar coating. If you are hosting a brunch or serving more than four people, double the recipe and cook in two batches.*

⅓ cup all-purpose flour

⅓ cup whole-wheat flour

3 tablespoons sugar, divided

½ teaspoon baking powder

¼ teaspoon ground cinnamon, plus ½ tablespoon

¼ teaspoon sea salt

2 tablespoons cold unsalted butter, cut into small pieces

¼ cup plus 1½ tablespoons whole milk

Nonstick cooking spray

**PREP TIME**
10 MINUTES

**TOTAL COOK TIME**
10 MINUTES

**AIR CRISP**
10 MINUTES

**ACCESSORIES**
COOK & CRISP™ BASKET, CRISPING LID

**NUT-FREE, VEGETARIAN, UNDER 30 MINUTES**

**TIP:** These tasty little bites are easy to customize with different flavors. Try swapping out the cinnamon for lemon zest and lavender, or top with confectioners' sugar.

1. Mix together the all-purpose flour, whole-wheat flour, 1 tablespoon of sugar, the baking powder, ¼ teaspoon of cinnamon, and the salt in a medium mixing bowl.

2. Use a pastry cutter or two forks to cut in the butter, breaking it up into little pieces until the mixture resembles coarse cornmeal. Add the milk and continue to mix together until the dough forms a ball.

3. Place the dough on a floured work surface and knead it until a smooth ball forms, about 30 seconds. Divide the dough into 8 equal pieces and roll each piece into a ball.

4. Place the Cook & Crisp Basket in the pot. Close the Crisping Lid. Preheat the unit by selecting Air Crisp, setting the temperature to 350°F, and setting the time to 3 minutes. Press Start/Stop to begin.

5. Coat the preheated Cook & Crisp Basket with cooking spray. Place the dough balls in the basket, leaving room between each, and spray them with cooking spray.

6. Close the Crisping Lid. Select Air Crisp, set the temperature to 350ºF, and set the time to 10 minutes. Press Start/Stop to begin.

7. In a medium mixing bowl, combine the remaining 2 tablespoons of sugar and ½ tablespoon of cinnamon.

8. When cooking is complete, toss the dough balls with the cinnamon sugar. Serve immediately.

**Per serving** Calories: 167; Total fat: 7g; Saturated fat: 4g; Cholesterol: 17mg; Sodium: 331mg; Carbohydrates: 25g; Fiber: 2g; Protein: 3g

# Apple Hand Pies

*There is a pie for every occasion. And while pie is delicious and beloved, there is something challenging about getting the perfect slice, let alone the perfect bite. Even America's favorite, apple pie, falls apart the second it hits the plate. But with a hand pie, the sweet apple and warm cinnamon filling is encased in a buttery, flaky piecrust for a delicious combination of flavors and textures in every bite. No fork required!*

**2 apples, peeled, cored, and diced**

**Juice of 1 lemon**

**3 tablespoons sugar**

**1 teaspoon vanilla extract**

**¼ teaspoon sea salt**

**1 teaspoon cornstarch**

**1 (2-crust) package refrigerated piecrusts, at room temperature**

**Nonstick cooking spray**

**PREP TIME**
15 MINUTES

**TOTAL COOK TIME**
24 MINUTES

**AIR CRISP**
24 MINUTES

**ACCESSORIES**
COOK & CRISP™ BASKET, CRISPING LID

**DAIRY-FREE, NUT-FREE, VEGAN, UNDER 30 MINUTES**

**TIP:** Use this recipe to turn all of your favorite pies into pocket-size snacks. Try peaches, cherries, or berries.

1. In a large mixing bowl, combine the apples, lemon juice, sugar, vanilla, and salt. Let the mixture stand for 10 minutes, then drain, reserving 1 tablespoon of the liquid.

2. In a small mixing bowl or glass, whisk the cornstarch into the reserved 1 tablespoon of liquid. Stir this mixture into the apple mixture.

3. Place the Cook & Crisp Basket in the pot and close the Crisping Lid. Preheat the unit by selecting Air Crisp, setting the temperature to 350ºF, and setting the time to 5 minutes. Press Start/Stop to begin.

4. Place the piecrusts on a lightly floured surface and cut them into 8 (4-inch-diameter) circles. Spoon 1 tablespoon of apple mixture into the center of each dough circle, leaving a ½-inch border. Brush the edges of the dough with water. Fold the dough over the filling and press the edges with a fork to seal.

5. Cut 3 small slits in the top of each pie. Coat each pie well with cooking spray and arrange 4 pies in the preheated Cook & Crisp™ Basket in a single layer.

6. Close the Crisping Lid. Select Air Crisp, set the temperature to 350°F, and set the time to 12 minutes. Press Start/Stop to begin. Once cooking is complete, check for your desired crispiness, then place the pies on a wire rack to cool.

7. Repeat steps 5 and 6 to cook the remaining hand pies.

**Per serving** Calories: 298; Total fat: 15g; Saturated fat: 6g; Cholesterol: 0mg; Sodium: 307mg; Carbohydrates: 40g; Fiber: 2g; Protein: 2g

# Strawberry Toaster Pastries

**SERVES 4**

*There is something inherently nostalgic about toaster pastries, not to mention that they are absolutely adorable. Flaky on the outside with warm jam on the inside, these homemade pastries are the grown-up versions of the ones I used to fight my brother for when we were growing up. While these tasty treats are branded as a breakfast food, I think they are much more of a dessert. That said, even brunch could use dessert!*

**1 refrigerated piecrust, at room temperature**

**¼ cup Simple Strawberry Jam (page 28)**

**Nonstick cooking spray**

**Vanilla icing, for frosting**

**Rainbow sprinkles, for topping**

**PREP TIME**
15 MINUTES

**TOTAL COOK TIME**
20 MINUTES

**AIR CRISP**
20 MINUTES

**ACCESSORIES**
COOK & CRISP™ BASKET, CRISPING LID

**DAIRY-FREE, NUT-FREE, VEGETARIAN, UNDER 30 MINUTES**

1. Place the Cook & Crisp Basket in the pot and close the Crisping Lid. Preheat the unit by selecting Air Crisp, setting the temperature to 350°F, and setting the time to 5 minutes.

2. On a lightly floured surface, roll out the piecrust into a large rectangle. Cut the dough into 8 rectangles.

3. Spoon 1 tablespoon of strawberry jam into the center of each of 4 dough rectangles, leaving a ½-inch border. Brush the edges of the filled dough rectangles with water. Top each with one of the remaining 4 dough rectangles. Press the edges with a fork to seal.

4. Carefully place the pastries in the preheated basket. Coat each pastry well with cooking spray and arrange 2 pastries in the Cook & Crisp Basket in a single layer.

5. Close the Crisping Lid and select Air Crisp, set the temperature to 350°F, and set the time to 10 minutes. Press Start/Stop to begin. Once cooking is complete, check for your desired crispiness, then place the pastries on a wire rack to cool. Repeat steps 1 through 5 with the remaining 2 pastries.

6. Frost the pastries with vanilla icing, then top with sprinkles.

**TIP:** Once you have the basics down, it is easy to customize the filling for everyone in the family. Try blueberry or raspberry jam instead of strawberry jam. Or skip the fruit altogether and combine brown sugar, cinnamon, and a little flour for a sugary-sweet filling.

**Per serving** Calories: 363; Total fat: 15g; Saturated fat: 6g; Cholesterol: 0mg; Sodium: 235mg; Carbohydrates: 55g; Fiber: 1g; Protein: 2g

# Campfire S'Mores

*For as long as I can remember, roasting marshmallows and singing songs or telling stories by a campfire is how the Swanhart family has spent summer evenings. I will always hold the time spent around the fire close to my heart. These Swanhart campfire s'mores made in the Ninja® Foodi™ have the creamy marshmallow, rich chocolate, and graham crackers that bring back all of my childhood memories—no fire required.*

**4 graham crackers**
**4 marshmallows**

**2 (1½-ounce) chocolate bars**

1. Place the Cook & Crisp Basket in the pot and close the Crisping Lid. Preheat the unit by selecting Air Crisp, setting the temperature to 350ºF, and setting the time to 5 minutes. Press Start/Stop to begin.

2. Break a graham cracker in half. Place half a chocolate bar on one half of the graham cracker. Add a marshmallow and top with the remaining graham cracker half to create a s'more. Repeat with the remaining ingredients to create 4 s'mores.

3. Using aluminum foil, wrap each s'more individually. Place all 4 foil-wrapped s'mores in the preheated Cook & Crisp Basket.

4. Close the Crisping Lid. Select Air Crisp, set the temperature to 350ºF, and set the time to 4 minutes. Press Start/Stop to begin.

5. When cooking is complete, carefully unwrap the s'mores and serve.

**Per serving** Calories: 152; Total fat: 7g; Saturated fat: 4g; Cholesterol: 0mg; Sodium: 50mg; Carbohydrates: 24g; Fiber: 1g; Protein: 1g

**PREP TIME**
10 MINUTES

**TOTAL COOK TIME**
4 MINUTES

**AIR CRISP**
4 MINUTES

**ACCESSORIES**
COOK & CRISP™ BASKET, CRISPING LID

**NUT-FREE, UNDER 30 MINUTES**

# Black and Blue Berry Crumble

**SERVES 6**

*A fruit crumble is a super-simple dessert option that works year-round. Berries and stone fruits scream summer, while apples are fabulous for fall. Use fresh fruit at the peak of the season, or use frozen fruit that you already have in the freezer. This recipe can be customized to make it your own, and it's so easy to make in the Ninja® Foodi™ that you'll wonder why you ever made it any other way.*

1 (16-ounce) package frozen blackberries

1 (16-ounce) package frozen blueberries

2 tablespoons cornstarch

½ cup water, plus 1 tablespoon

1 teaspoon freshly squeezed lemon juice

5 tablespoons granulated sugar, divided

½ cup all-purpose flour

½ cup rolled oats

⅔ cup brown sugar

⅓ cup cold unsalted butter, cut into pieces

1 teaspoon ground cinnamon

**PREP TIME**
10 MINUTES

**TOTAL COOK TIME**
30 MINUTES

**APPROX. PRESSURE BUILD**
8 MINUTES

**PRESSURE COOK**
10 MINUTES

**PRESSURE RELEASE**
2 MINUTES

**AIR CRISP**
10 MINUTES

**ACCESSORIES**
REVERSIBLE RACK, PRESSURE LID, CRISPING LID

**NUT-FREE, VEGETARIAN, UNDER 30 MINUTES**

1. Place the blackberries and blueberries in the Multi-Purpose Pan or a 1½-quart round ceramic baking dish.

2. In a small mixing bowl, stir together the cornstarch, 1 tablespoon of water, the lemon juice, and 3 tablespoons of granulated sugar. Pour this mixture over the fruit.

3. Place the pan on the Reversible Rack, making sure the rack is in the lower position. Cover the pan with aluminum foil. Pour the remaining ½ cup of water into the pot and add the rack with the pan to the pot. Assemble the Pressure Lid, making sure the pressure release valve is in the Seal position.

4. Select Pressure and set to High. Set the time to 10 minutes, then select Start/Stop to begin.

5. In a medium mixing bowl, combine the flour, oats, brown sugar, butter, cinnamon, and remaining 2 tablespoons of granulated sugar until a crumble forms.

**TIP:** This recipe uses frozen fruit, but you can easily use fresh fruit instead. Swap out the blackberries and blueberries for whatever you have on hand. Strawberries, raspberries, peaches, or apples, or a mix, would all be delicious in this recipe.

6. When pressure cooking is complete, quick release the pressure by moving the pressure release valve to the Vent position. Carefully remove the lid when the pressure has finished releasing.

7. Remove the foil and stir the fruit mixture. Evenly spread the crumble topping over the fruit.

8. Close the Crisping Lid. Select Air Crisp, set the temperature to 400°F, and set the time to 10 minutes. Select Start/Stop to begin. Cook until the top is browned and the fruit is bubbling.

9. When cooking is complete, remove the rack with the pan from the pot and serve.

**Per serving** Calories: 396; Total fat: 12g; Saturated fat: 7g; Cholesterol: 27mg; Sodium: 142mg; Carbohydrates: 72g; Fiber: 7g; Protein: 4g

# New York Cheesecake

SERVES 6

*My cheesecake bar is set pretty high. My grandma taught me how to make it years ago, and it is the only cake I request on my birthday. I tend to be a purist when it comes to the crust and filling. A crumbly graham cracker crust and a cream cheese and sour cream filling are the building blocks for the perfect cheesecake. I like mine plain, but you can top yours with Simple Strawberry Jam (page 28), caramel, or crumbled cookies.*

Nonstick cooking spray

1½ cups finely crushed graham crackers

4 tablespoons (½ stick) unsalted butter, melted

2 tablespoons granulated sugar

16 ounces cream cheese, at room temperature

½ cup light brown sugar

¼ cup sour cream

1 tablespoon all-purpose flour

½ teaspoon sea salt

1½ teaspoons vanilla extract

2 eggs

1 cup water

**PREP TIME**
15 MINUTES, PLUS 1 HOUR TO COOL AND 4 HOURS TO CHILL

**TOTAL COOK TIME**
1 HOUR

**APPROX. PRESSURE BUILD**
13 MINUTES

**PRESSURE COOK**
35 MINUTES

**PRESSURE RELEASE**
12 MINUTES

**ACCESSORIES**
REVERSIBLE RACK, PRESSURE LID

**NUT-FREE, VEGETARIAN**

1. Spray a 7-inch springform pan lightly with cooking spray. Cut a piece of parchment paper to fit the bottom of the pan and spray it with cooking spray. Cover the bottom of the pan tightly with aluminum foil so there are no air gaps.

2. In a medium mixing bowl, combine the graham cracker crumbs, butter, and granulated sugar. Press the mixture firmly into the bottom and up the side of the prepared pan.

3. Using a stand mixer or in a large bowl using an electric hand mixer, beat the cream cheese and brown sugar until combined. Add the sour cream and mix until smooth. Add the flour, salt, and vanilla, scraping down the side of the bowl as necessary.

4. Add the eggs and mix until smooth, being sure not to over-mix. Pour the cream cheese mixture into the prepared crust.

5. Pour the water into the pot. Place the springform pan on the Reversible Rack, making sure the rack is in the lower position. Place the rack in the pot.

6. Assemble the Pressure Lid, making sure the pressure release valve is in the Seal position. Select Pressure and set to High. Set the time to 35 minutes, then select Start/Stop to begin.

7. When pressure cooking is complete, allow the pressure to naturally release for 10 minutes, then quick release any remaining pressure by moving the pressure release valve to the Vent position. Carefully remove the lid when the pressure has finished releasing.

8. Remove the rack from the pot and let the cheesecake cool for 1 hour. Cover the cheesecake with foil and refrigerate to chill for at least 4 hours.

**Per serving** Calories: 551; Total fat: 39g; Saturated fat: 21g; Cholesterol: 781mg; Sodium: 627mg; Carbohydrates: 43g; Fiber: 1g; Protein: 9g

# Peanut Butter and Chocolate Lava Cakes

## SERVES 4

*If I could start every meal with dessert, I would, and while I love all desserts, I am partial to chocolate. When scanning a dessert menu, my eyes automatically go to the chocolate mousse or flourless chocolate cake. But if I see a dessert with chocolate and peanut butter? That is like icing on the cake. This recipe is a mash-up of my favorite things: Rich chocolate and ooey-gooey peanut butter!*

**Nonstick cooking spray**

**8 tablespoons (1 stick) unsalted butter, cut into pieces**

**¼ cup dark chocolate chips**

**¼ cup peanut butter chips**

**2 eggs**

**3 egg yolks**

**1¼ cups confectioners' sugar**

**1 teaspoon vanilla extract**

**½ cup all-purpose flour**

**PREP TIME**
15 MINUTES

**TOTAL COOK TIME**
20 MINUTES

**BAKE/ROAST**
20 MINUTES

**ACCESSORIES**
REVERSIBLE RACK, CRISPING LID

**VEGETARIAN, UNDER 30 MINUTES**

**TIP:** Take these cakes one step further and serve with a scoop of vanilla ice cream on the side.

1. Preheat the unit by selecting Bake/Roast, setting the temperature to 300°F, and setting the time to 5 minutes. Press Start/Stop to begin.

2. Meanwhile, grease 4 ramekins with cooking spray and set aside.

3. In a microwave-safe medium bowl, combine the butter, chocolate chips, and peanut butter chips. Microwave on high until melted, checking and stirring every 15 to 20 seconds.

4. Add the eggs, egg yolks, confectioners' sugar, and vanilla to the chocolate mixture and whisk until smooth. Stir in the flour a little at a time until combined and incorporated.

5. Divide the batter among the ramekins and wrap each with aluminum foil. Place the ramekins on the Reversible Rack, making sure the rack is in the lower position. Place the rack in the pot.

6. Close the Crisping Lid. Select Bake/Roast, set the temperature to 300°F, and set the time to 20 minutes. Select Start/Stop to begin.

7. When cooking is complete, remove the rack from the pot. Remove the foil and allow the ramekins to cool for 1 to 2 minutes.

8. Invert the lava cakes onto a plate and serve immediately.

**Per serving** Calories: 587; Total fat: 37g; Saturated fat: 21g; Cholesterol: 325mg; Sodium: 281mg; Carbohydrates: 52g; Fiber: 2g; Protein: 10g

# NINJA® FOODI™ COOKING TIME CHARTS

## PRESSURE COOK

### PRESSURE COOKING GRAINS

| GRAIN | AMOUNT | WATER | PRESSURE | COOK TIME | RELEASE |
|-------|--------|-------|----------|-----------|---------|
| For best results, rinse rice in a fine mesh strainer under cold water before cooking. | | | | | |
| Arborio rice | 1 cup | 3 cups | High | 7 mins | Natural |
| Basmati rice | 1 cup | 1 cup | High | 2 mins | Natural (10 mins) then Quick |
| Brown rice, short/ medium or long grain | 1 cup | 1¼ cups | High | 15 mins | Natural (10 mins) then Quick |
| Coarse grits/polenta* | 1 cup | 3½ cups | High | 4 mins | Natural (10 mins) then Quick |
| Farro | 1 cup | 2 cups | High | 10 mins | Natural (10 mins) then Quick |
| Jasmine rice | 1 cup | 1 cup | High | 2–3 mins | Natural (10 mins) then Quick |
| Kamut | 1 cup | 2 cups | High | 30 mins | Natural (10 mins) then Quick |
| Millet | 1 cup | 2 cups | High | 6 mins | Natural (10 mins) then Quick |
| Pearl barley | 1 cup | 2 cups | High | 22 mins | Natural (10 mins) then Quick |
| Quinoa | 1 cup | 1½ cups | High | 2 mins | Natural (10 mins) then Quick |
| Quinoa, red | 1 cup | 1½ cups | High | 2 mins | Natural (10 mins) then Quick |
| Spelt | 1 cup | 2½ cups | High | 25 mins | Natural (10 mins) then Quick |
| Steel-cut oats* | 1 cup | 3 cups | High | 11 mins | Natural (10 mins) then Quick |
| Sushi rice | 1 cup | 1½ cups | High | 3 mins | Quick |
| Texmati® rice, brown | 1 cup | 1¼ cups | High | 5 mins | Natural (10 mins) then Quick ➤ |

*After releasing pressure, stir for 30 seconds to 1 minute, then let sit for 5 minutes.

| GRAIN | AMOUNT | WATER | PRESSURE | COOK TIME | RELEASE |
|---|---|---|---|---|---|
| Texmati® rice, light brown | 1 cup | 1¼ cups | High | 2 mins | Natural (10 mins) then Quick |
| Texmati® rice, white | 1 cup | 1 cup | High | 2 mins | Natural (10 mins) then Quick |
| Wheat berries | 1 cup | 3 cups | High | 15 mins | Natural (10 mins) then Quick |
| White rice, long grain | 1 cup | 1 cup | High | 2 mins | Natural (10 mins) then Quick |
| White rice, medium grain | 1 cup | 1 cup | High | 3 mins | Natural (10 mins) then Quick |
| Wild rice | 1 cup | 1 cup | High | 22 mins | Natural (10 mins) then Quick |

## PRESSURE COOKING LEGUMES

| LEGUME | AMOUNT | WATER | PRESSURE | COOK TIME | RELEASE |
|---|---|---|---|---|---|
| **For best results, soak beans 8–24 hours before cooking.** | | | | | |
| Black beans | 1 lb | 6 cups | Low | 5 mins | Natural (10 mins) then Quick |
| Black-eyed peas | 1 lb | 6 cups | Low | 5 mins | Natural (10 mins) then Quick |
| Cannellini beans | 1 lb | 6 cups | Low | 3 mins | Natural (10 mins) then Quick |
| Cranberry beans | 1 lb | 6 cups | Low | 3 mins | Natural (10 mins) then Quick |
| Garbanzo beans (chickpeas) | 1 lb | 6 cups | Low | 3 mins | Natural (10 mins) then Quick |
| Great northern beans | 1 lb | 6 cups | Low | 1 min | Natural (10 mins) then Quick |
| Lentils (green or brown) | 1 cup dry | 2 cups | Low | 5 mins | Natural (10 mins) then Quick |
| Lima Beans | 1 lb | 6 cups | Low | 1 min | Natural (10 mins) then Quick |
| Navy beans | 1 lb | 6 cups | Low | 3 mins | Natural (10 mins) then Quick |
| Pinto beans | 1 lb | 6 cups | Low | 3 mins | Natural (10 mins) then Quick |
| Red kidney beans | 1 lb | 6 cups | Low | 3 mins | Natural (10 mins) then Quick |

# PRESSURE COOKING VEGETABLES

| VEGETABLE | AMOUNT | DIRECTIONS | WATER | ACCESSORY | PRESSURE | COOK TIME | RELEASE |
|---|---|---|---|---|---|---|---|
| Beets | 8 small or 4 large | Rinsed well, tops & ends trimmed; cool & peel after cooking | ½ cup | N/A | High | 15–20 mins | Quick |
| Broccoli | 1 head or 4 cups | Cut in florets, stem removed | ½ cup | Reversible Rack in steam position | Low | 1 mins | Quick |
| Brussels sprouts | 1 lb | Cut in half | ½ cup | Reversible Rack in steam position | Low | 1 mins | Quick |
| Butternut squash (cubed for side dish or salad) | 20 oz | Peeled, cut in 1-inch pieces, seeds removed | ½ cup | N/A | Low | 2 mins | Quick |
| Butternut squash (for mashed, puree, or soup) | 20 oz | Peeled, cut in 1-inch pieces, seeds removed | ½ cup | Reversible Rack in steam position | High | 5 mins | Quick |
| Cabbage (braised) | 1 head | Cut in half, then cut in ½-inch strips | ½ cup | N/A | Low | 3 mins | Quick |
| Cabbage (crisp) | 1 head | Cut in half, then cut in ½-inch strips | ½ cup | Reversible Rack in steam position | Low | 2 mins | Quick |
| Carrots | 1 lb | Peeled, cut in ½-inch pieces | ½ cup | N/A | High | 2–3 mins | Quick |
| Cauliflower | 1 head | Cut in florets, stem removed | ½ cup | N/A | Low | 1 mins | Quick |
| Collard greens | 2 bunches or 1 bag (16 oz) | Stems removed, leaves chopped | ½ cup | N/A | Low | 6 mins | Quick |
| Green Beans | 1 bag (12 oz) | Whole | ½ cup | Reversible Rack in steam position | Low | 0 mins | Quick ➤ |

| VEGETABLE | AMOUNT | DIRECTIONS | WATER | ACCESSORY | PRESSURE | COOK TIME | RELEASE |
|---|---|---|---|---|---|---|---|
| Kale leaves/ greens | 2 bunches or 1 bag (16 oz) | Stems removed, leaves chopped | ½ cup | N/A | Low | 3 mins | Quick |
| Potatoes, red (cubed for side dish or salad) | 2 lbs | Scrubbed, cut in 1-inch cubes | ½ cup | N/A | High | 1-2 mins | Quick |
| Potatoes, red (for mashed) | 2 lbs | Scrubbed, left whole | ½ cup | N/A | High | 15-20 mins | Quick |
| Potatoes, Russet or Yukon (cubed for side dish or salad) | 2 lbs | Peeled, cut in 1-inch cubes | ½ cup | N/A | High | 1-2 mins | Quick |
| Potatoes, Russet or Yukon (for mashed) | 2 lbs | Peeled, cut in 1-inch thick slices | ½ cup | N/A | High | 6 mins | Quick |
| Potatoes, sweet (cubed for side dish or salad) | 1 lb | Peeled, cut in 1-inch cubes | ½ cup | N/A | High | 1-2 mins | Quick |
| Potatoes, sweet (for mashed) | 1 lb | Peeled, cut in 1-inch thick slices | ½ cup | N/A | High | 6 mins | Quick |

## PRESSURE COOKING MEATS

| MEAT | WEIGHT | PREP | WATER | ACCESSORY | PRESSURE | COOK TIME | RELEASE |
|---|---|---|---|---|---|---|---|
| **Poultry** | | | | | | | |
| Chicken breasts | 2 lbs | Bone in | 1 cup | N/A | High | 15 mins | Quick |
| | 4 breasts (6-8 oz each) | Boneless | 1 cup | N/A | High | 8-10 mins | Quick |
| | Frozen, 4 large | Boneless | 1 cup | N/A | High | 25 mins | Quick |
| Chicken thighs | 8 thighs (4 lbs) | Bone in, skin on | 1 cup | N/A | High | 20 mins | Quick |
| | 8 thighs (4 lbs) | Boneless | 1 cup | N/A | High | 20 mins | Quick |

| MEAT | WEIGHT | PREP | WATER | ACCESSORY | PRESSURE | COOK TIME | RELEASE |
|---|---|---|---|---|---|---|---|
| Chicken, whole | 5–6 lbs | Bone in | 1 cup | Cook & Crisp™ Basket | High | 25–30 mins | Quick |
| Turkey breast | 1 breast (6–8 lbs) | Bone in | 1 cup | N/A | High | 40–50 mins | Quick |
| **Ground Meat** | | | | | | | |
| Ground beef, pork, or turkey | 1–2 lbs | Out of the package | ½ cup | N/A | High | 5 mins | Quick |
| Ground beef, pork, or turkey, frozen | 1–2 lbs | Frozen ground, not in patties | ½ cup | N/A | High | 20–25 mins | Quick |
| **Ribs** | | | | | | | |
| Pork baby back ribs | 2½–3½ lbs | Cut in thirds | 1 cup | N/A | High | 20 mins | Quick |
| **Roasts** | | | | | | | |
| Beef brisket | 3–4 lbs | Whole | 1 cup | N/A | High | 1½ hrs | Quick |
| Boneless beef chuck-eye roast | 3–4 lbs | Whole | 1 cup | N/A | High | 1½ hrs | Quick |
| Boneless pork butt | 4 lbs | Seasoned | 1 cup | N/A | High | 1½ hrs | Quick |
| Pork tenderloin | 2 tenderloins (1–1½ lbs each) | Seasoned | 1 cup | N/A | High | 3–4 mins | Quick |
| **Stew Meat** | | | | | | | |
| Boneless beef short ribs | 6 ribs (3 lbs) | Whole | 1 cup | N/A | High | 25 mins | Quick |
| Boneless leg of lamb | 3 lbs | Cut in 1-inch pieces | 1 cup | N/A | High | 30 mins | Quick |
| Boneless pork butt | 3 lbs | Cut in 1-inch cubes | 1 cup | N/A | High | 30 mins | Quick |
| Chuck roast, for stew | 2 lbs | Cut in 1-inch cubes | 1 cup | N/A | High | 25 mins | Quick |

# AIR CRISP

## 6.5 QUART

| INGREDIENT | AMOUNT | PREP | OIL | TEMP | COOK TIME | TOSS CONTENTS IN BASKET |
|---|---|---|---|---|---|---|
| **Vegetables** | | | | | | |
| Asparagus | 1 bunch | Whole, stems trimmed | 2 tsp | 390°F | 8–10 mins | Halfway through cooking |
| Beets | 6 small or 4 large (about 2 lbs) | Whole | None | 390°F | 45–60 mins | N/A |
| Bell peppers (for roasting) | 4 peppers | Whole | None | 400°F | 25–30 mins | Halfway through cooking |
| Broccoli | 1 head | Cut into florets | 1 tbsp | 390°F | 10–13 mins | Halfway through cooking |
| Brussels sprouts | 1 lb | Cut in half, | 1 tbsp | 390°F | 15–18 mins | Halfway through cooking |
| Butternut squash | 1–1½ lbs | Cut into 1- to 2-inch pieces | 1 tbsp | 390°F | 20–25 mins | Halfway through cooking |
| Carrots | 1 lb | Peeled, cut into ½-inch pieces | 1 tbsp | 390°F | 15 mins | Halfway through cooking |
| Cauliflower | 1 head | Cut into florets | 2 tbsp | 390°F | 15–20 mins | Halfway through cooking |
| Corn on the cob | 4 ears | Whole ears, husks removed | 1 tbsp | 390°F | 12–15 mins | Halfway through cooking |
| Green beans | 1 bag (12 oz) | Trimmed | 1 tbsp | 390°F | 7–10 mins | Halfway through cooking |
| Kale (for chips) | 6 cups, packed | Torn in pieces, stems removed | None | 300°F | 10 mins | Halfway through cooking |
| Mushrooms | 8 oz | Cut into ⅛-inch slices | 1 tbsp | 390°F | 7–8 mins | Halfway through cooking |
| Potatoes, Yukon gold and russet | 1½ lbs | Cut into 1-inch wedges | 1 tbsp | 390°F | 20–25 mins | Halfway through cooking |
| | 1 lb | Hand-cut, thin | ½–3 tbsp | 390°F | 20–25 mins | Halfway through cooking |
| | 1 lb | Hand-cut, thick | ½–3 tbsp | 390°F | 25 mins | Halfway through cooking |
| | 4 whole (6–8 oz each) | Pierced with fork 3 times | None | 390°F | 35–40 mins | N/A |

| INGREDIENT | AMOUNT | PREP | OIL | TEMP | COOK TIME | TOSS CONTENTS IN BASKET |
|---|---|---|---|---|---|---|
| Potatoes, sweet | 2 lbs | Cut into 1-inch chunks | 1 tbsp | 390°F | 15–20 mins | Halfway through cooking |
| | 4 whole (6-8 oz each) | Pierced with fork 3 times | None | 390°F | 35–40 mins | N/A |
| Zucchini | 1 lb | Cut length-wise into quarters, then cut into 1-inch pieces | 1 tbsp | 390°F | 15–20 mins | Halfway through cooking |
| **Poultry** | | | | | | |
| Chicken breasts | 2 breasts (¾–1½ lbs each) | Bone in | Brushed with oil | 375°F | 25–35 mins | N/A |
| | 2 breasts (½–¾ lb each) | Boneless | Brushed with oil | 375°F | 22–25 mins | N/A |
| Chicken thighs | 4 thighs (6-10 oz each) | Bone in | Brushed with oil | 390°F | 22–28 mins | N/A |
| | 4 thighs (4-8 oz each) | Boneless | Brushed with oil | 390°F | 18–22 mins | N/A |
| Chicken wings | 2 lbs | Drumettes & flats | 1 tbsp | 390°F | 24–28 mins | Halfway through cooking |
| Chicken, whole | 1 chicken (3-5 lbs) | Trussed | Brushed with oil | 375°F | 55–75 mins | N/A |
| **Beef** | | | | | | |
| Burgers | 4 patties (¼ lb each) | 1 inch thick | None | 375°F | 10–12 mins | Halfway through cooking |
| Steaks | 2 steaks (8 oz each) | Whole | None | 390°F | 10–20 mins | N/A |
| **Pork & Lamb** | | | | | | |
| Bacon | Up to 1 lb | Lay strips over basket | None | 325°F | 13–16 mins (no preheat) | N/A |
| Pork chops | 2 chops (10-12 oz each) | Thick cut, bone in | Brushed with oil | 375°F | 15–17 mins | Halfway through cooking |
| | 4 chops (6-8 oz each) | Boneless | Brushed with oil | 375°F | 15–18 mins | Halfway through cooking ➤ |

| INGREDIENT | AMOUNT | PREP | OIL | TEMP | COOK TIME | TOSS CONTENTS IN BASKET |
|---|---|---|---|---|---|---|
| Pork tenderloins | 2 tender-loins (1–1½ lbs each) | Whole | Brushed with oil | 375°F | 25–35 mins | Halfway through cooking |
| Sausages | 4 | Whole | None | 390°F | 8–10 mins | Turn/flip halfway through cooking |
| **Fish & Seafood** | | | | | | |
| Crab cakes | 2 cakes (6–8 oz each) | None | Brushed with oil | 350°F | 8–12 mins | N/A |
| Lobster tails | 4 tails (3–4 oz each) | Whole | None | 375°F | 7–10 mins | N/A |
| Salmon fillets | 2 fillets (4 oz each) | None | Brushed with oil | 390°F | 10–13 mins | N/A |
| Shrimp | 16 large | Whole, peeled, tails on | 1 tbsp | 390°F | 7–10 mins | N/A |
| **Frozen Foods** | | | | | | |
| Chicken nuggets | 1 box (12 oz) | None | None | 390°F | 12 mins | Halfway through cooking |
| Fish fillets | 1 box (6 fillets) | None | None | 390°F | 14 mins | Halfway through cooking |
| Fish sticks | 1 box (14.8 oz) | None | None | 390°F | 10 mins | Halfway through cooking |
| French fries | 1 lb | None | None | 360°F | 19 mins | Halfway through cooking |
| | 2 lbs | None | None | 360°F | 30 mins | |
| Mozzarella sticks | 1 box (11 oz) | None | None | 375°F | 8 mins | Halfway through cooking |
| Pot stickers | 1 bag (10 count) | None | Toss with 1 tsp oil | 390°F | 11–14 mins | Halfway through cooking |
| Pizza rolls | 1 bag (20 oz, 40 count) | None | None | 390°F | 12–15 mins | Halfway through cooking |
| Popcorn shrimp | 1 box (16 oz) | None | None | 390°F | 9 mins | Halfway through cooking |
| Tater Tots | 1 lb | None | None | 360°F | 20 mins | Halfway through cooking |

## AIR CRISP: 8 QUART

| INGREDIENT | AMOUNT | PREP | OIL | TEMP | COOK TIME | TOSS CONTENTS IN BASKET |
|---|---|---|---|---|---|---|
| **Vegetables** | | | | | | |
| Asparagus | 1 bunch | Whole, stems trimmed | 2 tsp | 390°F | 5–10 mins | Halfway through cooking |
| Beets | 6 small or 4 large (about 2 lbs) | Whole | None | 390°F | 45–60 mins | N/A |
| Bell peppers (for roasting) | 4 peppers | Whole | None | 400°F | 25–30 mins | Halfway through cooking |
| Broccoli | 1 head | Cut into florets | 1 tbsp | 390°F | 7–10 mins | Halfway through cooking |
| Brussels sprouts | 1 lb | Cut in half, stems removed | 1 tbsp | 390°F | 12–15 mins | Halfway through cooking |
| Butternut squash | 1–1½ lbs | Cut into 1- to 2-inch pieces | 1 tbsp | 390°F | 20–25 mins | Halfway through cooking |
| Carrots | 1 lb | Peeled, cut into ½-inch pieces | 1 tbsp | 390°F | 14–16 mins | Halfway through cooking |
| Cauliflower | 1 head | Cut into florets | 2 tbsp | 390°F | 15–20 mins | Halfway through cooking |
| Corn on the cob | 4 ears | Whole ears, husks removed | 1 tbsp | 390°F | 12–15 mins | Halfway through cooking |
| Green beans | 1 bag (12 oz) | Trimmed | 1 tbsp | 390°F | 5–6 mins | Halfway through cooking |
| Kale (for chips) | 6 cups, packed | Torn into pieces, stems removed | None | 300°F | 8–11 mins | Halfway through cooking |
| Mushrooms | 8 oz | Cut into ⅛-inch slices | 1 tbsp | 390°F | 5–7 mins | Halfway through cooking |
| Potatoes, Yukon gold and russet | 1½ lbs | Cut into 1-inch wedges | 1 tbsp | 390°F | 15 mins | Halfway through cooking |
| | 2 lbs | Hand-cut, thin | 2 tbsp | 390°F | 28 mins | Halfway through cooking |
| | 2 lbs | Hand-cut, thick | 2 tbsp | 390°F | 30 mins | Halfway through cooking |
| | 4 whole (6–8 oz each) | Pierced with fork 3 times | None | 390°F | 30–35 mins | N/A ➤ |

| INGREDIENT | AMOUNT | PREP | OIL | TEMP | COOK TIME | TOSS CONTENTS IN BASKET |
|---|---|---|---|---|---|---|
| Potatoes, sweet | 2 lbs | Cut into 1-inch chunks | 1 tbsp | 325°F | 15–20 mins | Halfway through cooking |
| | 4 whole (6–8 oz each) | Pierced with fork 3 times | None | 390°F | 30–35 mins | N/A |
| Zucchini | 1 lb | Cut length-wise into quarters, then cut into 1-inch pieces | 1 tbsp | 390°F | 15–20 mins | Halfway through cooking |
| **Poultry** | | | | | | |
| Chicken breasts | 2 breasts (¾–1½ lb. each) | Bone in | Brushed with oil | 375°F | 25–35 mins | N/A |
| | 2 breasts (½–¾ lb each) | Boneless | Brushed with oil | 375°F | 12–17 mins | N/A |
| Chicken thighs | 4 thighs (6–10 oz each) | Bone in | Brushed with oil | 390°F | 22–28 mins | N/A |
| | 4 thighs (4–8 oz each) | Boneless | Brushed with oil | 390°F | 18–22 mins | N/A |
| Chicken wings | 2 lbs | Drumettes & flats | 1 tbsp | 390°F | 25–30 mins | Halfway through cooking |
| Chicken, whole | 1 chicken (3–5 lbs) | Trussed | Brushed with oil | 375°F | 55–75 mins | Halfway through cooking |
| **Beef** | | | | | | |
| Burgers | 4 patties (¼ lb each) | 1 inch thick | None | 375°F | 8–10 mins | Halfway through cooking |
| Steaks | 2 steaks (8 oz each) | Whole | None | 390°F | 10–20 mins | N/A |
| **Pork & Lamb** | | | | | | |
| Bacon | 10 strips | Drape over Roasting Rack insert | None | 375°F | 10–15 mins | N/A |
| Lamb loin chops | 5 chops (¼ lb each) | 1 inch thick | Brushed with oil | 390°F | 8–12 mins | N/A |

| INGREDIENT | AMOUNT | PREP | OIL | TEMP | COOK TIME | TOSS CONTENTS IN BASKET |
|---|---|---|---|---|---|---|
| Pork chops | 2 chops (10–12 oz each) | Thick cut, bone in | Brushed with oil | 375°F | 15–17 mins | Halfway through cooking |
| | 4 chops (¼ lb each) | Thinly sliced, boneless | Brushed with oil | 375°F | 7–12 mins | Halfway through cooking |
| Pork tenderloins | 2 tender-loins (1–1½ lbs each) | Whole | Brushed with oil | 375°F | 25–35 mins | Halfway through cooking |
| Sausages | 4 sausages | Whole | None | 390°F | 8–10 mins | Turn/flip halfway through cooking |
| **Fish & Seafood** | | | | | | |
| Crab cakes | 2 cakes (6–8 oz each) | None | Brushed with oil | 350°F | 10–15 mins | N/A |
| Lobster tails | 4 tails (3–4 oz each) | Whole | None | 375°F | 5–7 mins | N/A |
| Salmon fillets | 2 fillets (4 oz each) | None | Brushed with oil | 390°F | 6–10 mins | N/A |
| Shrimp | 16 large | Whole, peeled, tails on | 1 tbsp | 390°F | 5–7 mins | N/A |
| **Frozen Foods** | | | | | | |
| Chicken nuggets | 1 box (12 oz) | None | None | 390°F | 12 mins | Halfway through cooking |
| Egg rolls | 4 egg rolls | None | None | 390°F | 12 mins | N/A |
| Fish fillets | 1 box (6 fillets) | None | None | 390°F | 14 mins | Halfway through cooking |
| Fish sticks | 1 box (14.8 oz) | None | None | 390°F | 10 mins | Halfway through cooking |
| French fries | 1 lb | None | None | 360°F | 19 mins | Halfway through cooking |
| Mozzarella sticks | 1 box (11 oz) | None | None | 375°F | 8 mins | Halfway through cooking |
| Onion rings | 1 bag (16 oz) | None | None | 390°F | 8 mins | Halfway through cooking ➤ |

| INGREDIENT | AMOUNT | PREP | OIL | TEMP | COOK TIME | TOSS CONTENTS IN BASKET |
|---|---|---|---|---|---|---|
| Pot stickers | 1 bag (24 oz, 20 count) | None | None | 390°F | 12–14 mins | Halfway through cooking |
| Pizza rolls | 1 bag (20 oz, 40 count) | None | None | 390°F | 12 mins | Halfway through cooking |
| Shrimp, breaded | 1 box (9 oz, 12 count) | None | None | 390°F | 9 mins | Halfway through cooking |

## STEAM

| INGREDIENT | AMOUNT | PREP | LIQUID | COOK TIME |
|---|---|---|---|---|
| **Vegetables** | | | | |
| Asparagus | 1 bunch | Whole spears | 2 cups | 7–15 mins |
| Broccoli | 1 crown or 1 (12-oz) bag | Cut into florets | 2 cups | 5–9 mins |
| Green beans | 1 (12-oz) bag | Whole | 2 cups | 6–12 mins |
| Brussels sprouts | 1 lb | Whole, trimmed | 2 cups | 8–17 mins |
| Carrots | 1 lb | Cut into 1-inch pieces | 2 cups | 7–12 mins |
| Cabbage | 1 head | Cut into wedges | 2 cups | 6–12 mins |
| Cauliflower | 1 head | Cut into florets | 2 cups | 5–10 mins |
| Corn on the cob | 4 | Whole, husks removed | 2 cups | 4–9 mins |
| Kale | 1 (16-oz) bag | Trimmed | 2 cups | 7–10 mins |
| Sugar snap peas | 1 lb | Whole pods, trimmed | 2 cups | 5–8 mins |
| Potatoes | 1 lb | Peeled and cut into 1-inch pieces | 2 cups | 12–17 mins |
| Spinach | 1 (16-oz) bag | Whole leaves | 2 cups | 3–7 mins |
| Butternut squash | 24 oz | Peeled, cut into 1-inch cubes | 2 cups | 10–15 mins |
| Sweet potatoes | 1 lb | Cut into ½-inch cubes | 2 cups | 8–14 mins |
| Zucchini or summer squash | 1 lb | Cut into 1-inch slices | 2 cups | 5–10 mins |
| **Eggs** | | | | |
| Poached eggs | 4 | In ramekin or silicone cup | 1 cup | 3–6 mins |

# DEHYDRATE

| FOOD LOAD | PREP | TEMP | DEHYDRATE TIME |
|---|---|---|---|
| **Fruits & Vegetables** | | | |
| Apple chips | Core removed, sliced ⅛ inch thick, rinsed in lemon water | 135°F | 7–8 hrs |
| Asparagus | Washed and cut into 1-inch pieces; blanched | 135°F | 6–8 hrs |
| Bananas | Peeled, cut into ⅜-inch pieces | 135°F | 8–10 hrs |
| Beet chips | Peeled, cut into ⅛-inch pieces | 135°F | 7–8 hrs |
| Eggplant | Peeled, sliced ¼ inch thick; blanched | 135°F | 6–8 hrs |
| Fresh herbs | Rinsed, patted dry, stems removed | 135°F | 4–6 hrs |
| Gingerroot | Cut into ⅜-inch pieces | 135°F | 6 hrs |
| Mangos | Peeled, cut into ⅜-inch pieces | 135°F | 6–8 hrs |
| Mushrooms | Cleaned with soft brush—do not wash | 135°F | 6–8 hrs |
| Pineapple | Cored, peeled, and sliced ⅜ inch to ½ inch thick | 135°F | 6–8 hrs |
| Strawberries | Halved or sliced ½ inch thick | 135°F | 6–8 hrs |
| Tomatoes | Washed and sliced ⅜ inch thick or grated. Steam if you plan to rehydrate. | 135°F | 6–8 hrs |
| **Meats** | | | |
| All jerky (not salmon) | Cut into ¼-inch slices, follow jerky recipe in the Inspiration Guide that came with your Foodi™ | 150°F | 5–7 hrs |
| Salmon jerky | Cut into ¼-inch slices, follow jerky recipe in the Inspiration Guide that came with your Foodi™ | 165°F | 5–8 hrs |

# MEASUREMENTS AND CONVERSIONS

## VOLUME EQUIVALENTS (LIQUID)

| US STANDARD | US STANDARD (OUNCES) | METRIC (APPROXIMATE) |
| --- | --- | --- |
| 2 tablespoons | 1 fl. oz. | 30 mL |
| ¼ cup | 2 fl. oz. | 60 mL |
| ½ cup | 4 fl. oz. | 120 mL |
| 1 cup | 8 fl. oz. | 240 mL |
| 1½ cups | 12 fl. oz. | 355 mL |
| 2 cups or 1 pint | 16 fl. oz. | 475 mL |
| 4 cups or 1 quart | 32 fl. oz. | 1 L |
| 1 gallon | 128 fl. oz. | 4 L |

## VOLUME EQUIVALENTS (DRY)

| US STANDARD | METRIC (APPROXIMATE) |
| --- | --- |
| ⅛ teaspoon | 0.5 mL |
| ¼ teaspoon | 1 mL |
| ½ teaspoon | 2 mL |
| ¾ teaspoon | 4 mL |
| 1 teaspoon | 5 mL |
| 1 tablespoon | 15 mL |
| ¼ cup | 59 mL |
| ⅓ cup | 79 mL |
| ½ cup | 118 mL |
| ⅔ cup | 156 mL |
| ¾ cup | 177 mL |
| 1 cup | 235 mL |
| 2 cups or 1 pint | 475 mL |
| 3 cups | 700 mL |
| 4 cups or 1 quart | 1 L |

## OVEN TEMPERATURES

| FAHRENHEIT (F) | CELSIUS (C) (APPROXIMATE) |
| --- | --- |
| 250° | 120° |
| 300° | 150° |
| 325° | 165° |
| 350° | 180° |
| 375° | 190° |
| 400° | 200° |
| 425° | 220° |
| 450° | 230° |

## WEIGHT EQUIVALENTS

| US STANDARD | METRIC (APPROXIMATE) |
| --- | --- |
| ½ ounce | 15 g |
| 1 ounce | 30 g |
| 2 ounces | 60 g |
| 4 ounces | 115 g |
| 8 ounces | 225 g |
| 12 ounces | 340 g |
| 16 ounces or 1 pound | 455 g |

# THE DIRTY DOZEN™ AND
# THE CLEAN FIFTEEN™

A nonprofit environmental watchdog organization called Environmental Working Group (EWG) looks at data supplied by the U.S. Department of Agriculture (USDA) and the Food and Drug Administration (FDA) about pesticide residues. Each year it compiles a list of the best and worst pesticide loads found in commercial crops. You can use these lists to decide which fruits and vegetables to buy organic to minimize your exposure to pesticides and which produce is considered safe enough to buy conventionally. This does not mean they are pesticide-free, though, so wash these fruits and vegetables thoroughly.

## DIRTY DOZEN

apples
celery
cherries
grapes
nectarines
peaches
pears
potatoes
spinach
strawberries
sweet bell peppers
tomatoes

*Additionally, nearly three-quarters of **hot pepper** samples contained pesticide residues.

## CLEAN FIFTEEN

asparagus
avocados
broccoli
cabbages
cantaloupes
cauliflower
eggplants
honeydew melons
kiwis
mangoes
onions
papayas
pineapples
sweet corn
sweet peas (frozen)

# INDEX

# ACKNOWLEDGMENTS

First and foremost, thank you to Julien, my best friend, my faithful taste tester, my cameraman, and my husband. Thank you for supporting me, even when it means that I am writing a cookbook in the months leading up to our wedding, and for having faith in me.

To my friends and family, thank you for your words of encouragement and for cheering me on throughout this journey. I am so thankful to have each and every one of you in my corner.

To my amazing team at Ninja: Corey, Judy, Sam, Meghan, Alex, and Meg, thank you for inspiring me every day. Thank you for supporting my wild ideas, for making me excited to come to work, and for filling the world with flavorful recipes.

To Justin Warner, thank you for consulting on this project, for pushing me and the team outside of our comfort zone, and for authoring the forward to this book. You have been an instrumental part of the team and I am humbled by your kind words.

To Talia and my team at Callisto Media, thank you for joining me on this journey and for believing in this product. I am so happy to be working with you again and am proud to be part of the Callisto Media family.

Last but never least, to my readers, thank you for trying my recipes and sharing them with your friends and loved ones. I hope you love the Ninja® Foodi™ and these recipes as much as I do!

# ABOUT THE AUTHOR

 **Kenzie Swanhart** is an author, food blogger, and culinary professional whose focus is on bringing simple recipes with real ingredients to her readers. With more than 100,000 copies of her cookbooks sold, Kenzie never wavers in her mission: Creating and sharing easy yet flavorful recipes made with real ingredients with her readers.

As the head of culinary marketing and innovation for Ninja, a leading kitchen appliance company, Kenzie and her team provide a unique, food-first point of view for the development of new products and recipes to make consumers' lives easier and healthier. You'll also see her serving as the face of Ninja on a leading television home shopping network, where she shares tips, tricks, and recipes for the company's full line of products.

Kenzie lives in Boston with her husband, Julien, and their dog, Charlie.

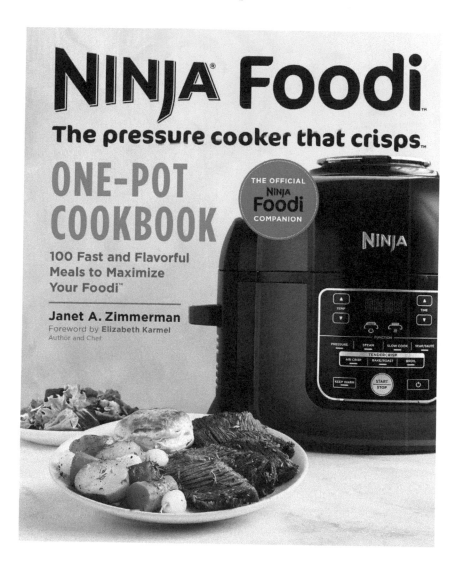

CPSIA information can be obtained
at www.ICGtesting.com
Printed in the USA
LVHW01s0826260818
587852LV00001B/1/P